transforming
homosexuality

transforming homosexuality

WHAT THE BIBLE SAYS ABOUT SEXUAL ORIENTATION AND CHANGE

Denny Burk

Heath Lambert

P U B L I S H I N G
P.O. BOX 817 • PHILLIPSBURG • NEW JERSEY 08865-0817

Unless otherwise indicated, Scripture quotations are from the ESV® Bible (The Holy Bible, English Standard Version®), copyright © 2001 by Crossway, a publishing ministry of Good News Publishers. Used by permission. All rights reserved.

Unless otherwise indicated, the Scripture translations in chapters 3 and 6 are the authors' own.

Scripture quotations marked (NASB) are from the NEW AMERICAN STANDARD BIBLE®. ©Copyright The Lockman Foundation 1960, 1962, 1963, 1968, 1971, 1972, 1973, 1975, 1977. Used by permission.

Note from the NET Bible® copyright ©1996–2006 by Biblical Studies Press, L.L.C. All rights reserved.

Italics within Scripture quotations indicate emphasis added.

Typesetting by Samuel Craig

ISBN: 978-1-59638-139-1 (pbk)
ISBN: 978-1-59638-146-9 (ePub)
ISBN: 978-1-59638-147-6 (Mobi)

Printed in the United States of America

Library of Congress Cataloging-in-Publication Data

Burk, Denny.
 Transforming homosexuality : what the Bible says about sexual orientation and change / Denny Burk, Heath Lambert.
     pages cm
 Includes bibliographical references.
 ISBN 978-1-59638-139-1 (pbk.) -- ISBN 978-1-59638-146-9 (epub) -- ISBN 978-1-59638-147-6 (mobi)
 1. Homosexuality--Religious aspects--Christianity. 2. Sexual orientation--Religious aspects--Christianity. 3. Change (Psychology)--Religious aspects--Christianity. I. Title.
 BR115.H6B875 2015
 241'.664--dc23
                          2015032664

But if you consent to evil desires and haven't struggled against them, you will have to bewail your defeat; and I hope you do bewail it, or you may lose all sense of sorrow. . . . What we long for, of course, is that these evil desires should not even well up from our flesh. But as long as we are living here, we are unable to bring this about.

—*Augustine, Sermon 152 on Romans 7:25–8:3*

But thanks be to God that though you were slaves of sin, you became obedient from the heart to that form of teaching to which you were committed, and having been freed from sin, you became slaves of righteousness.

—*The Apostle Paul, Romans 6:17–18* (NASB)

Contents

Foreword

The modern secular consensus is that an individual's pattern of sexual attraction, whether heterosexual or homosexual, should be accepted as a given and considered normal. More than that, the secular view demands that this pattern of sexual orientation be accepted as integral to an individual's identity. According to the secular consensus, any effort to change an individual's sexual orientation is essentially wrong and harmful. The contemporary therapeutic worldview is virtually unanimous in this verdict, but nothing could be more directly at odds with the gospel of Jesus Christ.

The New Testament reveals that a homosexual sexual orientation, whatever its shape or causation, falls out of line with the Creator's purpose for humanity. All sinners who are saved by the Lord Jesus Christ know the need for the redemption of our bodies—including our sexual selves. But those with a homosexual sexual orientation face another dimension to this reality: they also need a fundamental reordering of their sexual attraction. About this, the Bible is clear.

But the issue here is not merely undoing same-sex attraction. Christians know that heterosexuals are just as in need of sexual redemption as homosexuals. The Bible and the testimony of the gospel point us to the cross of Christ and to the sinner's fundamental need for redemption, not for mere moral improvement. Further, the Bible offers no hope for any human ability to change our sinful desires—only the power of the gospel can do that.

The believer in the Lord Jesus Christ receives the forgiveness of sins, the gift of eternal life, and the righteousness of Christ imputed by faith. But the redeemed Christian is also united with Christ, indwelt by the Holy Spirit, and given means of grace through, for example, the preaching of the Word of God. The Bible reveals that God conforms believers to the image of Christ, doing that work within the human heart that sinful humans cannot do themselves. The Bible reveals that believers are to grow into Christlikeness, knowing that this growth is a progressive process that ends with their eventual glorification at the end of the age. In this life, we know a process of growing more holy, more sanctified, and more obedient to Christ. In the life to come, we will know perfection as Christ glorifies his church.

This means that Christians cannot accept any argument suggesting the impossibility of fundamentally reorienting a believer's desires in such a way that increasingly pleases God and is increasingly obedient to Christ. To the contrary, we must argue that this process is exactly what the Christian life is to demonstrate. As Paul writes, "Therefore, if anyone is in Christ, he is a new creation. The old has passed away; behold, the new has come" (2 Corinthians 5:17).

The Bible is also honest about the struggle to overcome sin and sinful desires. Paul writes about this in Romans 7, but the exhortations of the entire New Testament also make this clear. Christians who experience same-sex attraction must know that these desires are sinful. Thus, faithful Christians who struggle with these desires must know that God wants both their affections and their patterns of attraction reordered according to his Word. All Christians struggle with their own patterns of sinful desires, sexual and otherwise. Our responsibility as Christians is to be obedient to Christ, knowing that only he can save us from ourselves.

These are challenging theological issues and represent one of the urgent pastoral tasks of our time. This is why Denny Burk and Heath Lambert's new book, *Transforming Homosexuality: What the Bible Says about Sexual Orientation and Change*, is such a tremendous gift to the church. These men are scholars of the highest caliber with pastoral hearts. Further, in this book Burk and Lambert keep the hope of the gospel and Christ's cross and resurrection at the very center of their counsel. Something as deeply entrenched as a pattern of sexual attraction is not easily changed—our doctrine of sin explains that—but we do know that with Christ all things are possible.

Christians know that believers among us struggle to submit their sexual desires to Christ. This is not something true only of those whose desires are homosexual. It is true of all Christians. Yet we know that those believers who are struggling to overcome homosexual desires have a special struggle—one that requires the full conviction and support of the body of Christ. We will see the glory of God in the growing obedience of Christ's redeemed people. And, along with the apostle Paul and all the redeemed, we will await the glory that is yet to be revealed to us.

R. ALBERT MOHLER JR.

Why Do We Need This Book?

This is not a typical Christian book about homosexuality.

Most Christian books on homosexuality deal with the topic of homosexual behavior and what the Bible says about its sinfulness. These books are important. As our culture continues to devolve on this matter, the biblical teaching has come under growing attack. For millennia, Christians have believed and taught that the Scriptures sanction sexual activity only in the context of marriage between one man and one woman for life. They have held that any sexual desire or behavior outside of marriage is sinful. This understanding has certainly been the case for homosexual behavior, which is condemned in every single passage of Scripture that addresses it. We affirm that interpretation of Scripture,[1] and have even written about it.[2] We are thankful for our brothers and sisters in Christ who continue to articulate biblical fidelity about homosexual behavior.[3] We pray for them and desire to encourage them in their work. Our task here, however, is different in two ways.

Our goal is not to consider, again, the ethics of homosexual behavior, but to consider the ethics of homosexual desire, often referred to as homosexual orientation. Faithful Christians are united in their rejection of homosexual behavior. However, there is not as much clarity when it comes to issues of orientation or same-sex attraction. The goal of our work in this book is to establish from Scripture that desires for a sinful act are sinful precisely because the desired act is sinful. We will carefully define same-sex attraction and show from the Bible why it is sinful.

There is another element of our book that is different from other books treating the topic of homosexuality. Almost every Christian book on this topic focuses exclusively on ethics. And, whether we are discussing desires or behavior, the matter of ethics is crucial. We must know which desires and behaviors are sinful and which ones are righteous. Ethics, however, is not the only challenge confronting the church today. Another pressing reality is ministry. People who struggle with homosexual desires and behaviors need to change. They need to experience progress in holiness. That is why this book also focuses on helping our brothers and sisters in Christ to know how to pursue this change. Biblical change means transformation into the image of Christ (2 Cor. 3:18). What the Bible commands, therefore, is not heterosexuality, but holiness (Eph. 1:4).

We write this book as men who are concerned about sexuality in general. We have both written books on the ethics of sexuality and on ministering to those with sexual problems.[4] Quite frankly, sex is important. It is the source of intense joy and profound pain. We desire to help the church think more deeply about the important issues of human sexuality.

We also write this book as men with concerns about the direction of our culture concerning homosexuality in particular. Most Christians have been surprised by the velocity of cultural change on the issue of homosexuality. Just one measure of that change is the acceptance of homosexual marriage. In 2005, same-sex marriage was illegal in every state in America. In 2015, the Supreme Court of the United States has declared same-sex marriage to be a constitutional right nationwide.[5] That is a tremendous amount of change for one decade. There has never been a period of human history in which the church has confronted such a challenge as this one. Our desire in these dark days is to help the church to embrace the light of Christ on these crucial matters.

We also offer this book as men with concerns about the evangelical response to the important issue of homosexual orientation. Faithful Christians are resisting the cultural tide and affirming the traditional teachings of Scripture on the matter of homosexual behavior. The issue of orientation, however, has thrown the church a curveball. As the church encounters modern "insights" about homosexual orientation, many are struggling to come to terms with what should be believed and taught. New ideas about sexuality are where loyalty to Christ is being tested in our time. It is one thing when a young Christian has not been taught well on these issues and needs discipleship and correction. But it is quite another thing when a professing believer embraces a studied rejection of Christ's word. In our day, beliefs about sexuality have become a line dividing sheep from goats. We cannot overemphasize the fact that the stakes really are that high, and our rendering of sexual orientation is a big part of that discussion. We want to contribute to the church's growing wisdom on this matter as we move together toward biblical fidelity on this crucial issue.

We desire for this book to bring about change. That is the reason we titled it *Transforming Homosexuality*. We want people who have struggled with homosexual desire to know the transforming power of Jesus Christ, which leads to holiness. The Bible teaches that transformed behavior grows out of transformed thinking (Rom. 12:2; Eph. 4:23; Col 3:10). Because this is true, we believe that the best way for people to be transformed in their experience of homosexuality is to be transformed in their thinking about homosexuality. We need the grace of Jesus Christ to bind our consciences to his Word and to gift us with this transformation. It is our prayer that he would use this book as one means to provide this gift.

Part One of this work focuses on the ethics of desire. Chapter one defines sexual orientation and offers a critique of the idea that it is a morally neutral concept. Chapter two explores how the Bible's teaching about temptation, desire, and sin maps onto the concepts of sexual orientation and same-sex attraction. Part Two of our book explains how people experiencing same-sex attraction might experience transformation. Chapter three clears away five common "myths" about what that transformation looks like. Chapter four charts a path of transformation based on repentance. Chapter five concludes with some ways that the church needs to "transform" its own ways of thinking about and of ministering to those with same-sex attraction.

This book is offered with the conviction that sexuality is a wonderful gift from our sovereign God that is to be enjoyed within the context of marriage. We are heartbroken by the pain and turmoil that people experience when they attempt to obtain the joys of sexuality outside the marital bond. Our modest work here is offered with the prayer that the glory of God would be manifest in the transformed lives of his covenant people and that this book would play at least some small part in that great work.

Questions for Reflection

1. What can happen when homosexuality is viewed exclusively in light of ethics to the exclusion of ministry to individuals?
2. How can one guard against the tendency to view heterosexuality as the solution to homosexuality instead of personal holiness?
3. How has the rapid cultural acceptance of homosexuality impacted the church's perspective on this issue?
4. How does transformed behavior grow out of transformed thinking? (See Rom. 12:2, Eph. 4:23, Col. 3:10.)

PART ONE

The Ethics of Desire

What Is Same-Sex Attraction?

Arriving at biblical clarity on the important issue of same-sex attraction and homosexual orientation requires precision in our use of terms. Some of the disagreement among evangelicals about the sinfulness of homosexual orientation has been a result of people talking past one another and using unclear language. We want to avoid that confusion by clearly defining our terms.

Same-Sex Attraction and Orientation

The most important term is *orientation*. It is crucial to understand the meaning behind this term. Orientation is a newer concept with a very specific and secular genesis. For this reason, we will access the definition of *orientation* used by the American Psychological Association (APA). Our decision to use the APA's definition has some qualifications, however, so we want to make a few comments about the APA and our use of their definition.

First, as Christians committed to Scripture, we confess that our authority is God's Word, which has been inscripturated for us in the books of the Old and New Testaments. No authority, no matter how widely accepted or scientific it is, can eclipse the authority of Scripture in defining the norms of Christian belief and practice. We are not using the APA's definition of *orientation* because we believe its authority eclipses that of the Scriptures.

Second, the APA is a very secular authority. The APA has adopted a secular, unbiblical view, which affirms homosexual behavior. As people committed to the authority of Scripture, we are profoundly concerned that the APA would embrace a practice that causes so much turmoil and is at odds with human flourishing. We do not use the APA's definition because we embrace their secular and unbiblical worldview. To the contrary, we reject it.

Third, the APA has a habit of changing its positions to fit with shifting cultural views. That is particularly the case with this issue of homosexuality.[1] In other words, what the APA articulates about homosexuality today is not what it has articulated in the past, and is not necessarily what it will articulate in the future. We do not use the APA's definition because it has been—or can be expected to be—a reliable voice on this matter. In fact, we have concerns about its use of the term *orientation*, which we will make clear below.

Fourth, our use of the APA's definition should not imply that we accept sexual orientation as a biblical way of describing human identity. As will be clear below, we believe that sexual-orientation ideology ignores God's revealed purpose in creating us as sexual beings and reduces human identity to the sum total of fallen human desire. Rosaria Butterfield has written powerfully to this point: "Words, like kitchen washrags, carry and distribute history (and bacteria) with each use, and the category invention of sexual orientation brings much bacteria with it. Everyone loses when we define ourselves using categories that God does not."[2]

With all these concerns, then, why would we access their definition? The reason, quite frankly, is because we need to explain what people commonly mean by the term *sexual orientation*. To that end, we thought it useful to access a definition that is widely accepted by those on all sides of this issue. The APA's definition does indeed reflect what many people believe sexual orientation to be. That is why it is an apt starting point for our biblical evaluation of the concept.

With that in mind, let us consider the APA's definition.

Sexual orientation refers to an enduring pattern of emotional, romantic, and/or sexual attractions to men, women, or both sexes. Sexual orientation also refers to a person's sense of identity based on those attractions, related behaviors, and membership in a community of others who share those attractions.[3]

According to this established way of speaking, the experience of an orientation is the experience of certain kinds of attractions. A homosexual orientation is comprised of various attractions to persons of the same sex as oneself. There are several different aspects of this definition, which we will unpack below. For now, we can summarize this definition by saying that a person with a homosexual orientation experiences same-sex sexual attractions and same-sex emotional attractions and may choose to identify in community with others who experience these attractions.

Four Approaches to Same-Sex Attraction and Behavior

As we write this book, four different approaches to same-sex attraction and behavior have emerged in the broader "Christian" dialogue on these topics. We place *Christian* in quotes because we are not convinced that all these approaches are faithfully Christian. Still, the persons representing these positions profess a connection with the Christian tradition. Though some of them are clearly not writing in submission to Scripture, it is important to understand their positions and the contributions they are making to the conversation that believers in Jesus are having about these issues. We do not mean to give a comprehensive survey of the literature on this subject. Nor do we wish to imply that these categories never overlap in a given personality.[4] We are simply trying to sketch the contours of current conversations about homosexuality.

Liberal

The first approach to same-sex attraction and behavior is an approach that compromises Christian faithfulness on the issue. This group professes to be working within the Christian tradition but disavows the biblical teaching on this matter. For its proponents, Scripture is not the *norma normans* of the church's life because the Scripture can be normed by our own experiences and opinions. New Testament scholar Luke Timothy Johnson typifies this approach and has stated in no uncertain terms his repudiation of the Bible's authority:

> I have little patience with efforts to make Scripture say something other than what it says, through appeals to linguistic or cultural subtleties. The exegetical situation is straightforward: we know what the text says. But what are we to *do* with what the text says? . . .
>
> I think it important to state clearly that we do, in fact, reject the straightforward commands of Scripture, and appeal instead to another authority when we declare that same-sex unions can be holy and good. And what exactly is that authority? We appeal explicitly to the weight of our own experience and the experience thousands of others have witnessed to, which tells us that to claim our own sexual orientation is in fact to accept the way in which God has created us. By so doing, we explicitly reject as well the premises of the scriptural statements condemning homosexuality— namely, that it is a vice freely chosen, a symptom of human corruption, and disobedience to God's created order.[5]

We have at least one thing in common with Johnson. We, too, have little patience with those who do hermeneutical gymnastics with Scripture in order to obscure or eliminate the Bible's clear condemnations of homosexual behavior. But where we disagree profoundly is on what we should do with the Scripture's teaching on this matter. Ironically, Johnson and others in this group often interpret the meaning of Scripture in a way similar to those who hold the traditional view. The crucial difference is that this group has no problem saying the Bible is wrong whenever it says that homosexuality is sinful. No Christian embracing the authority and sufficiency of God's Word could ever embrace a view so recklessly dismissive of the sacred Scriptures.

Revisionist

The second approach to same-sex attraction is also one that compromises Christian faithfulness even though it does so a bit differently. Whereas the liberal approach openly opposes the teachings of Scripture, the revisionist attempts to accommodate the Scriptures to the practice of homosexuality. The effort of these revisionists is, therefore, to reinterpret the classic texts of Scripture that teach against homosexuality and to make it seem as though they do not speak to the experience of homosexuals in contemporary culture. One argument says that because the Bible does not address homosexuality as we know it today, the Bible's prohibitions are irrelevant.[6] This is the view of Matthew Vines in *God and the Gay Christian: The Biblical Case in Support of Same-Sex Relationships*.

> The bottom line is this: The Bible doesn't directly address
> the issue of same-sex *orientation*—or the expression of that
> orientation. While its six references to same-sex behavior
> are negative, the concept of same-sex behavior in the Bible is
> sexual excess, not sexual orientation.[7]

For Vines, the Bible does not condemn those homosexual practices that are the overflow of loving commitment. The Bible condemns only displays of homosexual practice that are based on excessive lust. This argument is unpersuasive for reasons that we have articulated elsewhere.[8] We will say here only that the interpretations offered by Vines and others are an unbiblical and unchristian attempt to revise biblical teaching that two millennia of Christians have found to be clear and compelling. It would be quite something if Christians living in the last four decades had been able to figure something out that everyone else had missed.

Neo-Traditional

The approach of the third group is very different from that of the first two. Many persons adopting a neo-traditional approach are our brothers and sisters in Christ. Even though we ultimately disagree with their understanding of these issues, we are grateful for their desire to think through these matters from the stand-point of Christian faithfulness. Neo-traditionalists embrace the Bible as authoritative and affirm the historical understanding of scriptural teaching about homosexual behavior. Where the neo-traditionalists differ is on the subject of same-sex attraction. This group wants to argue that there is nothing explicitly sinful about a homosexual orientation, *per se*. Many of the writers at the Spiritual Friendship blog represent this view.[9] Some of the writers there are Roman Catholic,[10] but many of the contributors are Protestant, including New Testament scholar Wesley Hill. Hill has been a winsome and articulate spokesperson for this view, and in an article titled "Is Being Gay Sanctifiable?" he tries to show that there are valuable aspects of being gay. In that article he interacts with the suggestion that all sexual sin, including homosexuality and lesbianism, must be mortified.

> My main worry with some of the "renunciation" and "sur-render" and "death to self" language that Christians use in

relation to homosexuality is that, for most people, it will end up implying that we believe all aspects of "being gay" are sinful. This is a devastating burden for many same-sex attracted Christians to bear, since it then leaves them trying to parse, ever more minutely and obsessively, how much of their desires for friendship, intimacy, companionship, community, etc. are a result of their sexual orientation. Then, if they think that those desires *are* a result of their same-sex attraction, they're left feeling that they must repent of things that, surely, God intends for blessing and good in their lives—and things that have a rich history of commendation and sanctification in the history of the Church.[11]

It is worth noting here that we would agree that same-sex attraction is in a certain sense sanctifiable, and we will argue for that later in this book. When Hill states that it is sanctifiable, however, he means something different than we do. For Hill, to sanctify being gay means to find praiseworthy elements of the orientation and to channel those into good spiritual fruit. Hill explains,

> My sexuality, my basic erotic orientation to the world, is inescapably intertwined with how I go about finding and keeping friends. . . . Rather than interpreting my sexuality as a license to go to bed with someone or even to form a monogamous sexual partnership with him, I can harness and guide its energies in the direction of sexually abstinent, yet intimate, friendship. . . . My being gay and saying no to gay sex may lead me to be *more* of a friend to men, not less.[12]

Hill affirms the sinfulness of homosexual behavior but wants to find spiritual benefits to same-sex attraction. We love

Wesley Hill and are thankful for his commitment to Scripture and chastity. We are deeply concerned about his argument, however. Sexual attraction to a person of the same sex is not a platform for spiritual fruit. It is an occasion for repentance. We would take the classic Christian approach that sanctifying homosexual desires means that those desires can be mortified and that new, holy desires can grow in their place (Rom. 8:13). Our burden in this book is to demonstrate that Christians should not give quarter to any vestige of homosexuality, whether behavior or desire.

Traditional

The traditional view is the one we will advocate in this book. Our view is the one of historic Christianity, which sees both homosexual behavior and homosexual desires as sinful. We do not mean to claim that every Christian in the history of the church has articulated things as we have here. We do mean to claim, however, that what we argue in this book is not novel. Our argument has deep roots that can be traced back to the Protestant Reformers, to Augustine, and to the apostle Paul.[13] We also believe that sinful desires and behaviors can be changed by the power of God's grace in Jesus Christ. We do not mean to imply that same-sex–attracted Christians will be freed from every inclination to sin in this life. Perfectionism is an errant view of sanctification for straight people, and it is no less so for gay people as well. Nevertheless, we do believe that the gospel provides resources for real progress in holiness over the course of a believer's life. That is the biblical norm for all Christians, including ones who experience ongoing struggles with same-sex sexual attraction. The Christian Scriptures are able to interact with, understand, and provide norms for the novel understanding of homosexual orientation that the church is facing today. It is able to do this with the relevance that only its ancient wisdom can add to this contemporary discussion. More than this, Jesus' powerful resurrection from the grave communicates real power to people struggling with desires that feel hopelessly ingrained.

Evaluating Same-Sex Orientation

So what is sexual orientation? And does the Bible give us any resources for evaluating the concept?[14] As we mentioned above, we are using the APA's definition of sexual orientation as the starting point for our evaluation.

> Sexual orientation refers to an enduring pattern of emotional, romantic, and/or sexual attractions to men, women, or both sexes. Sexual orientation also refers to a person's sense of identity based on those attractions, related behaviors, and membership in a community of others who share those attractions.[15]

In previous writing on same-sex orientation, we have focused almost entirely on the first part of this definition—sexual attraction. We still believe that focus is justified, because the sexual attraction component is the foundation for everything else in the definition. But still, there are other aspects of the definition that cannot be ignored. The definition includes the emotional/romantic aspects of attraction. The definition also specifies sexual orientation as an identity category. Our evaluation must include these components as well. So we will render a brief evaluation of these three components in the APA's definition of orientation: sexual attraction, emotional/romantic attraction, and identity.

Same-Sex Orientation as Sexual Attraction

Same-sex sexual attraction is the feature that most people connect with having a homosexual orientation. It may be that same-sex orientation includes more than sexual attraction, but it certainly does not mean less than that.[16] Most writers identify enduring experiences of sexual desire for persons of the same sex as the defining feature of a same-sex orientation. We could multiply examples of this, but one secular instance appears in Simon LeVay's 2011 book *Gay, Straight, and the Reason Why: The Science of Sexual Orientation*. He writes,

> Sexual orientation has to do with the sex of our preferred sex partners. More specifically, it is the trait that predisposes us to experience sexual attraction to people of the same sex as ourselves (*homosexual, gay,* or *lesbian*), to persons of the other sex (*heterosexual* or *straight*), or to both sexes (*bisexual*).[17]

Notice that the central element in this definition is the direction of a person's sexual attractions. The author goes on to list other, non-sexual elements of attraction. Nevertheless, the defining feature is the sexual one. Those who have an enduring experience of sexual desire for persons of the same sex are said to have a homosexual orientation. Edward Stein also writes from a secular perspective and contends that "sexual orientation has to do with a person's sexual desires and the sexual activities in which he or she is disposed to engage."[18]

Writing from a Christian point of view, Mark Yarhouse and Erica Tan likewise define orientation in terms of sexual desire.

> When we discuss *sexual orientation* . . . we are referring to what is often thought to be a more enduring pattern of attraction to another based on one's sexual desire. . . . Orientation is often discussed in our cultural context as heterosexual (sexual desire as attraction to the opposite sex), homosexual (to the same sex) and bisexual (to both sexes).[19]

This is the common way that the terms are used—sexual orientation is defined by the direction of one's sexual desire over time.[20]

We will argue that, because the Bible speaks clearly about our sexual desires and attractions, it also renders a clear word about this defining element of sexual orientation. We can put this in practical terms with respect to homosexuality. When individuals feel themselves experiencing an attraction or a desire toward a person of the same sex, the Bible is clear about their responsibility before God at that point. In the next chapter, we will show that Jesus teaches that it is always sinful to desire something that God forbids (Matt. 5:27–28). The very experience of the desire becomes an occasion for repentance. And it is pastoral malpractice to tell someone who is feeling a sexual attraction for a person of the same sex that there is no need to repent. In the moment when the feeling of sexual desire is aroused in such a way—in that moment—that person must confess the desire as sinful and turn from it. A person is not absolved of an immoral sexual desire simply because it seems to follow an enduring pattern—i.e., an orientation. The enduring nature of same-sex desire is an indication not that God approves such desire but that we are intractably sinful apart from grace. It is on these terms that John and Paul Feinberg render this verdict on sexual orientation: "We stand firmly committed to the position that Scripture teaches that homosexual and lesbian orientation and behavior are contrary to the order for human sexuality God placed in creation. Hence they are sinful."[21]

A common objection to the foregoing goes like this: "If a person cannot control whether he has same-sex attraction, how can that attraction be considered sinful?" This objection bases moral accountability upon whether one has the ability to choose his proclivities. But this is not how the Bible speaks of sin and judgment. There are all manner of predispositions that we are

born with and that we experience as unchosen realities.[22] Nevertheless, the Bible characterizes such realities as sin: pride, anger,
anxiety, just to name a few. Why would we put same-sex attraction in a different category from those other predispositions that
we groan to be delivered from and that we are called to repent
of? Jesus says that all such sins proceed from the heart and that
we are therefore morally accountable for them (Mark 7:21). And
this assessment is in no way mitigated by the possibility that
we come by it naturally. Whether same-sex attraction derives
from nature or from nurture (or both) is not strictly relevant to
our moral evaluation of the *fact* of homosexual attraction.[23] As
Richard Hays writes,

> The Bible's sober anthropology rejects the apparently com-
> monsense assumption that only freely chosen acts are mor-
> ally culpable. Quite the reverse: the very nature of sin is that
> it is *not* freely chosen. That is what it means to live "in the
> flesh" in a fallen creation. We are in bondage to sin but still
> accountable to God's righteous judgment of our actions. In
> light of this theological anthropology, it cannot be main-
> tained that a homosexual orientation is morally neutral
> because it is involuntary.[24]

Hays is correct. The issue really isn't a new one. At the end of
the day, our moral assessment of sexual attraction forces us back
onto terrain that has been well traversed by theologians over
the past twenty centuries. The matter really does come down
to one's anthropology.

If you view human nature as a blank slate, and if you reduce
sin to one's behavior—that which one chooses to do—then you
are going to assess the morality of same-sex sexual attraction
in a certain way. If, however, you regard the human condition

as fundamentally flawed—that we are sinful not only in our choices but also in our nature—then you are going to approach the matter in a different way. And that difference goes back at least as far as Augustine and Pelagius. And the evangelical tradition—especially in its Reformed expressions—has sided definitively with Augustine.

We will show in the next chapter that our moral assessment of homosexuality does not depend upon its being chosen. All sinful desire springs spontaneously from our nature, but even if it is something unchosen, that does not make it any less sinful. To that end, Charles Hodge contends that our pre-behavioral dispositions—which are often unchosen—have a moral character to them. This view of the matter stands squarely in opposition to "Pelagian and Rationalistic Doctrine." He writes,

> We do attribute moral character to principles which precede all voluntary action and which are entirely independent of the power of the will. . . . We hold ourselves responsible not only for the deliberate acts of the will, that is, for acts of deliberate self-determination, which suppose both knowledge and volition, but also for emotional, impulsive acts, which precede all deliberation; and not only for such impulsive acts, but also for the principles, dispositions, or immanent states of the mind, by which its acts whether impulsive or deliberate, are determined. When a man is convinced of sin, it is not so much for specific acts of transgression that his conscience condemns him, as for the permanent states of his mind; his selfishness, worldliness, and maliciousness; his ingratitude, unbelief, and hardness of heart; his want of right affections, of love to God, of zeal for the Redeemer, and of benevolence towards men. These are not acts. They are not states of mind under control of the will; and yet in

the judgment of conscience, which we cannot silence or pervert, they constitute our character and are just ground of condemnation.[25]

Hodge doesn't leave it there. He makes a scriptural argument for this view and concludes, "The denial, therefore, that dispositions or principles as distinguished from acts, can have a moral character, subverts some of the most plainly revealed doctrines of the sacred Scriptures."[26] The key doctrine he has in mind is the doctrine of original sin. On this point, Hodge writes,

> All Christian churches receive the doctrines of original sin and regeneration in a form which involves not only the principle that dispositions, as distinguished from acts, may have a moral character, but also that such character belongs to them whether they be innate, acquired, or infused. It is, therefore, most unreasonable to assume the ground that a man can be responsible only for his voluntary acts, or for their subjective effects, when our own consciousness, the universal judgment of men, the word of God, and the Church universal, so distinctly assert the contrary.[27]

Hodge's key point is this: we are sinners by nature and by choice. At the most fundamental level, in fact, our nature produces our choices.[28] We inherit a sinful nature from our father Adam so that we are spring-loaded to sin.[29] And that is not merely a word for people experiencing same-sex attraction. That is a word for all of us. Same-sex attraction is merely one variety of fallenness. But it is not the only one. We are all fallen and are in this predicament together.

Hodge's account of sin and of the nature of man is not an outlier. It represents the mainstream of evangelical—and especially

Reformed—anthropology.[30] The Reformed tradition elaborated Augustine's view on this point and specified that original sin means that all humanity inherits both Adam's guilt and his sinful nature. Inheriting Adam's sinful nature means that every person is born into a state of total depravity that can be remedied only by the redemption found in Christ. That depravity manifests itself in a heart that is naturally and sinfully at odds with God and his law. The Christian is someone whose nature has been renewed by the Holy Spirit and who is no longer in bondage to indwelling sin. Nevertheless, even the Christian has to wrestle against a sinful nature that is not completely eradicated until the resurrection of the body. This means that our experience of sinful desire/attraction is often involuntary and unchosen, arising spontaneously from our sinful nature.

We believe this evangelical anthropology to be the scriptural position. Modern attempts to remove same-sex sexual attraction—or even same-sex orientation—from this biblical framework are doomed to failure. They produce a superficial understanding of sin and of the human condition, and they hinder people from perceiving their need for the transformation that Jesus provides.

Same-Sex Orientation as Emotional and Romantic Attraction

What are we to make of emotional and romantic components of attraction to the same sex? Are they sinful in the same way that the desire for homosexual sex is sinful? Some writers claim that they are not and that the non-sexual components of same-sex attraction can be holy and pleasing to God. Wesley Hill, for example, argues that same-sex attraction cannot be reduced to a desire for same-sex genital contact.[31] He argues that same-sex attraction also includes a desire for same-sex friendship and even a "preference" for same-sex companionship.[32] We do not deny that same-sex–attracted persons report heightened emotional connections with persons of the same sex and that they perceive those connections as part of their attractions. Nevertheless, the defining element of same-sex attraction is desire for a sexual relationship with someone of the same sex. When same-sex sexual desire is removed from the equation, then we are no longer talking about same-sex attraction—at least not in the sense that modern people mean the term. When modern people talk about same-sex attraction, they intend a kind of attraction that includes sexual possibility between persons of the same sex. They do not mean to label as *gay* every person capable of emotional bonds with a person of the same sex. It is the same-sex sexual desire that is the constitutive element.

One might find parallels between the non-sexual bonds of a gay couple and the non-sexual bonds of straight same-sex friends. But even though there are parallels, there is a crucial distinction. The bonds of affection between straight friends do not contain within them sexual possibility. In cases where such erotic possibilities are not present, we are simply not talking about what the APA means by *homosexual orientation*. The bonds of affection between David and Jonathan or Jesus and John, for example, did not contain sexual possibility. The same is not true of the bonds of affection between gay couples. In fact, those bonds are defined in part *by* their sexual possibility. To the degree that same-sex bonds are defined by sexual possibility and intention, they are sinful.

What, then, are we to make of the emotional bonds that gay people experience for persons of the same sex? Can those attractions be sanctified?[33] Yes, they can. They can be sanctified when they are shorn of the elements that otherwise make them sinful. When sexual possibility and intention are removed through repentance and faith toward God, there can exist the real bonds of holy, God-honoring same-sex friendship. But those bonds can be cultivated only when we recognize that the desire for sinful sex can never be the foundation for holy friendships. Holy friendships are the fruit of chastity in both thought and deed. All Christians should desire to have close same-sex relationships. We should not tarnish the sanctity of these same-sex friendships by locating them on a continuum with homosexuality—a category that has always been understood as one at odds with chastity.[34] Same-sex–attracted people can have holy friendships with persons of the same sex. When they do, desire for homosexual sex has been overcome, and the remaining bonds of affection can in no sense be labeled homosexual, gay, or same-sex attracted.

Same-Sex Orientation as Identity

The APA's definition also speaks of same-sex orientation as a "person's sense of identity." That identity is based squarely on same-sex sexual attraction and on membership in a community that shares those attractions. How do we evaluate sexual orientation in terms of identity?

We should note that even though the APA's clinical definition speaks of sexual orientation as identity, that concept has been vigorously contested by queer theorists. For example, Hanne Blank argues in her book *Straight: The Surprisingly Short History of Heterosexuality* that the terms *heterosexual* and *homosexual* are "neologisms" of the modern era. She writes, "These terms came to exist because a need was perceived to identify people as representatives of generic types distinguished on the basis of their tendencies to behave sexually in particular ways."[35] In this sense neither homosexuality nor heterosexuality are fixed identity markers. Rather, they are socially constructed terms, and people's sexual proclivities are in actuality more variable than we have been led to believe.[36] It is ironic that, just as many evangelicals are coming to embrace the notion of sexual orientation, queer theorists are rejecting it as a fixed identity marker.

But it is not just queer theorists who are destabilizing the concept of orientation as identity. In an important 2014 article in *First Things*, Michael Hannon contends that the concept of sexual orientation as identity actually undermines the teleological tradition of Christian sexual ethics. In other words, he argues that over the last 150 years the West has allowed "sexual orientations" to replace the "teleological tradition with a brand new creation."[37] Under the new regime, a person's identity would no longer be conceived in terms of a Creator's purpose but in terms of one's personal sense of attraction to either or both sexes. In this way the natural law tradition has given way to "psychiatric normality" and has paved the way for a new sexual ethic based on sexual orientation identities.[38] Hannon thus concludes, "The role of Christian chastity today, I argue, is to dissociate the Church from the false absolutism of identity based upon erotic tendency."[39] In short: in God's world, we are who God says we are. We are not merely the sum total of our fallen sexual desires.

For these reasons, same-sex orientation as an identity category is problematic. From a Christian perspective, it invites us to embrace fictional identities that go directly against God's revealed purposes for his creation. It invites us to define ourselves and the meaning of our lives according to the sum total of our fallen sexual attractions. A Christian approach to these realities is very different. Sam Allberry's description of his own experience with same-sex attraction is very helpful.

> The kind of sexual attractions I experience are not fundamental to my identity. They are part of *what I feel* but are not *who I am* in a fundamental sense. I am far more than

my sexuality. . . . Desires for things God has forbidden are
a reflection of how sin has distorted me, not how God has
made me.[40]

God's purposes for us are obscured if we make our sinful
sexual attractions the touchstone of our being. God gives us a
bodily identity that indicates his purposes for us sexually, and
those purposes are unambiguously ordered to the opposite sex
within the covenant of marriage. To embrace an identity that
goes against God's revealed purpose is by definition sinful.[41] It
is for this reason that Rosaria Butterfield warns Christians that
sexual orientation ideology is at odds with a Christian view of the
human person. On this point, it is worth quoting her at length.

> There is no ontological category of sexual orientation. The
> idea of identity emerging from sexual desire embodies a
> philosophy of the soul that is false. . . . Christians who feel
> beholden by culture to use the concept of sexual orienta-
> tion ought to stop and ask one question: where ought we to
> situate sexual orientation in relation to biblical principles?
> If we were to fish around for a biblical place to contain this
> neologism (which is sloppy theology at best), it could only be
> traced to the biblical concept of "flesh."[42]

We agree with Butterfield on this crucial point. Accepting sexual orientation as an identity-defining element of the human
condition is foreign to Scripture—except as a feature of human
sinfulness. For this reason, the term *orientation* may be altogether
irredeemable for Christians trying to communicate biblical truth
about how God has created us as bearers of his image. When
Christians use terms like "gay Christian" to describe believers
who experience same-sex attraction, they are speaking in a way

that is at best misleading and at worst a complete surrender to the falsehoods of the sexual revolution. We are not to define ourselves as the sum total of fallen sexual desire. We are to define ourselves according to the purposes that God has revealed in his word.

When we say that ours is the traditional view grounded in classical Christianity, we mean that ours is the biblically consistent way to apply a Christian understanding of human sinfulness and human nature to this contemporary discussion of homosexual desires and behavior. We want to demonstrate that this is the case in the pages that follow.

Questions for Reflection

1. According to each of the four approaches to same-sex attraction and behavior, what authority does the Bible have in addressing this subject?

2. Is the sinfulness of our sexual attractions dependent on whether or not we choose them?

3. How does understanding the different aspects of sexual orientation (sexual attraction, emotional and romantic attraction, and identity) help when we are ministering to people with same-sex attraction?

2

Is Same-Sex Attraction Sinful?

Is same-sex attraction sinful?[1] We realize that even to ask the question raises eyebrows. In fact, we have found that to raise the issue in such terms arouses suspicions of people on both sides of the larger cultural debate over the ethics of homosexuality. On one side, you have those who view sexual orientation as an unchosen, immutable attribute that has no more moral dimension to it than does skin color or eye color. Same-sex orientation is simply another element of human diversity to be acknowledged and celebrated and certainly not to be stigmatized. For those who hold this view, we might as well be asking, "Is it sinful to have brown hair?" For them, it is offensive and uncouth even to ask the question.

On the other side, you have those who believe that homosexuality is a choice and that even to grant the existence of something called "sexual orientation" is to concede too much to the sexual revolutionaries. On this view, if you grant that certain people are born with same-sex attractions, then you cannot hold someone responsible for acting on those attractions. For some Christians, the category of sexual orientation would overturn the logic of the Bible's clear prohibition of same-sex behavior. So even to ask the question "Is same-sex orientation sinful?" raises the hackles of both sides of the debate.

We would also acknowledge the existence of another group who might have a negative response to this question. And perhaps this group is on the ascent right now in conservative circles of the evangelical movement. Today you will find many evangelicals willing to grant the distinction between same-sex attraction and same-sex behavior. And among those who do, they are very clear that Scripture treats same-sex behavior as sinful. But many of them are reluctant to say that same-sex attraction *itself* is sinful. They are rightly concerned about placing an undue burden of guilt upon chaste Christians who, nevertheless, continue to experience ongoing same-sex attraction. These dear brothers and sisters struggle faithfully and practice chastity, but they sense that they cannot eliminate same-sex attractions that well up within them spontaneously and uninvited. So it seems cruel and unusual to call their unchosen and unwanted attractions sinful. To call their attractions sinful while they are otherwise living a life of faithfulness and chastity seems to confuse temptation with sin. It seems to load these brothers and sisters up with burdens too heavy for them to bear. And no one wants to sin against them and fall under the censure that Jesus laid against the scribes and Pharisees: "And they tie up heavy loads, and lay them on men's shoulders; but they themselves are unwilling to move them with so much as a finger" (Matthew 23:4).

So we understand that the question as we have posed it immediately puts friends and foes of the gospel on their guard. Nevertheless, it is a question that evangelical Christians cannot dodge. And it is a question that many evangelicals have not yet thought their way through to biblical clarity. For this reason, we have a great need to let the Bible's message illuminate our thinking about these categories.

The aim of this chapter is to explore whether the Bible's teaching about temptation, sin, and desire maps onto the experience of same-sex attraction. What does the Bible have to say about the pre-behavioral components of sexual sin? Can someone feel an attraction for something sinful without the attraction itself becoming sinful? Can a person experience ongoing desire and inclination for sexual sin without those desires and inclinations themselves becoming sinful? There are those who argue that our sexual desires, attractions, and inclinations are of no moral consequence as long as we do not act on them. On this basis, therefore, homosexual orientation and even same-sex sexual attraction are treated as benign elements of the human personality. But is this really what the Bible teaches?

In looking at these issues, we need to understand at the outset that we are not having a discussion about how many angels can dance on the head of a pin. Rather, we are discussing an issue with immediate practical and pastoral implications. How we answer these questions has a profound impact on how we invite our gay and lesbian neighbors to come to Christ. Our answer will also define how same-sex–attracted brothers and sisters pursue a faithful walk with Christ. We would also argue that our answer informs how opposite-sex–attracted brothers and sisters should pursue a faithful walk with Christ. The stakes are high, and we need to get this right.

What Makes Desire Sinful?

The terms *same-sex attraction* and *sexual orientation* may be modern inventions, but discussions about the pre-behavioral components of our sin are not. Christians have been sorting out what God's revelation has to say about this question for two millennia. From the earliest centuries of the church until now, Christians have been coming to terms with scriptural teaching on the morality of sexual desire. Biblically speaking, not all sexual desire is evil. But neither is it all good. On what basis can we tell the difference? Looking at the New Testament, we might focus on any number of terms that fit within the semantic range of "desire." Louw and Nida's Greek lexicon includes twenty-one different entries under the semantic domain "Desire Strongly."[2] In the history of Christian thought, however, two of these terms have been central to the discussion: *epithumeō* and *epithumia*, which are the Greek verb and noun for "desire."

A Historical Perspective

The centrality of these terms owes in no small part to Augustine's magisterial contribution to the doctrine of original sin. A touchstone of that doctrine is a concept that Augustine calls *concupiscence*, a term that derives from the Latin translation of the biblical terms for "desire" mentioned above. Augustine sought to account for not only the sinful deeds that we commit but also for the desire that produces those deeds. He labeled that desire *concupiscence* and sought to explain from Scripture how Christians should think about their own indwelling attraction to sin.

The heretic Pelagius—a contemporary of Augustine—denied that human beings inherit the sin of Adam. Pelagius and his followers held that we are sinful only insofar as we make sinful choices and that we do not inherit a sinful nature from Adam. Augustine famously contended against the error of Pelagianism in favor of a thoroughgoing doctrine of original sin. He argued that every human being ever born (except One) inherits both Adam's guilt and Adam's sinful nature. That sinful nature consists not merely of sinful deeds, but also of sinful desire and inclination (also known as "concupiscence"). It may be the case that Augustine's earlier views stopped short of calling concupiscence sin. But his later writings tell a different story, as he eventually reaches the conclusion that concupiscence itself is sinful. He concludes that it is not just sinful deeds that are sinful, but it is also the desire that gives birth to those deeds that is sinful.[3] This principle is true for all sin, but Augustine applies it specifically to sexual sin. Commenting on Romans 7:20, Augustine says that the apostle Paul calls concupiscence sin: "He gives the name of sin, you see, to that from which all sins spring, namely to the lust [concupiscence] of the flesh."[4] Likewise, in a sermon that Augustine preached in 419 on Romans 7:15–25, he writes,

> This lust [desire/concupiscence] is not, you see—and this is a point you really must listen to above all else: you see, this lust is not some kind of alien nature. . . . It's our debility, it's our vice. It won't be detached from us and exist somewhere else, but it will be cured and not exist anywhere at all [in the resurrection].[5]

Augustine makes a similar remark in "On Marriage and Concupiscence," where he argues that fallen desire is sin. He writes, "By a certain manner of speech it is called sin, since it arose from sin, and, when it has the upper hand, produces sin, the guilt of it prevails in the natural man. . . . Arising from sin, it is, I say, called sin."[6] Augustine understands "desire" to be the key pre-behavioral component of our sin, and that desire consists of the fallen inclinations that we all continually experience before ever actually choosing to sin.

Augustine's influence over subsequent Christian reflection on this point cannot be overestimated. Although Augustine sometimes refrained from calling concupiscence sin, his mature reflection on Scripture reveals that he did, indeed, label it as such. The Roman Catholic tradition, however, reflects the view that concupiscence is not itself sin, and that only conscious acts of the will can truly be deemed to be sinful.[7] This explains why the *Catechism of the Catholic Church* calls homosexual behavior sinful but stops short of calling homosexual desire sinful and instead labels the desire as "objectively disordered."[8] The Reformed tradition differs sharply from Roman Catholicism on this point and reflects the Augustinian view that both evil desire and evil deeds must be regarded as thoroughly sinful.[9] Perhaps the classic expression of this comes from John Calvin, who also acknowledges his explicit appropriation of Augustine on the point in 3.3.10 of his *Institutes*:

> We hold that there is always sin in the saints, until they are freed from their mortal frame, because depraved concupiscence resides in their flesh, and is at variance with rectitude. Augustine himself does not always refrain from using the name of sin, as when he says, "Paul gives the name of sin to that carnal concupiscence from which all sins arise. This in regard to the saints loses its dominion in this world, and is destroyed in heaven." In these words he admits that believers, in so far as they are liable to carnal concupiscence, are chargeable with sin.[10]

Jesus' Perspective

Augustine certainly has framed this discussion for the ages, but it is not his exposition of *epithumeō* and *epithumia* that is decisive. These particular terms for "desire" are paradigmatic primarily because of Jesus' use of the verb form in the Sermon on the Mount, where he prohibits not only sinful sexual deeds but also sinful sexual desire. The NASB translation is a typical literal rendering of this text: "You have heard that it was said, 'You shall not commit adultery'; but I say to you, that everyone who looks on a woman to lust for her has committed adultery with her already in his heart" (Matt. 5:27–28). Some readers observe the purpose construction in Jesus' words, "in order to lust for her." Because of the purpose clause, they conclude that unintentional desire for adultery is not sin. But this is a false conclusion. Jesus is connecting the seventh commandment ("you shall not commit adultery") to the tenth commandment ("you shall not covet"). And the tenth commandment prohibits not merely *intentional* desire for adultery, but *all* desire for adultery, without respect to the voluntary/involuntary nature of the desire. Considering the fact that the Mosaic law requires sacrifices for unintentional sin, it is not difficult to see that the *chosenness* of a desire does not ultimately determine its sinfulness. The sinfulness of a desire is determined solely by its conformity or lack of conformity to the law of God.[11]

Matthew's version of Jesus' saying in 5:27 quotes directly from the Greek version of Exodus 20:14 and Deuteronomy 5:18, which is simply the seventh commandment's prohibition on adultery. So when Jesus follows with a word about *looking at a woman to lust for her*, he is specifically addressing the *sex desire* that contemplates adultery.[12] He is talking about the pre-behavioral component of the sin of adultery. Desire, in this sense, is a *longing* or a *craving* for sexual sin.

But this raises a question: what is the difference between a morally harmless desire and a lustful desire? Some people wonder if the issue has to do with the intensity of desire. For them, a slight and passing desire for another man's wife is not the sin that is in view. It is only a high level of sexual desire that Jesus identifies as sinful lust. Others wonder if the key issue is the *chosenness* of the desire. In this view, it is only when one chooses to look at another man's wife with the intent to lust for her that it is sinful. But are these distinctions biblical? Is Jesus exempting low-level sexual desire for another man's wife while prohibiting only lustful desire? Is the bottom-line issue whether or not the one lusting *chooses* to feel the way that he feels?

In some ways, these questions are provoked not by the terms that Jesus uses but by the English words we use to translate them.[13] Jesus is using the verb *epithumeō*, which simply means *to desire* something.[14] It denotes the idea of *longing* or *craving* for some object. The term is variously used in the Bible with either the negative connotation of *lust* or the neutral connotation of *desire*. But the difference between sinful *lust* and benign *desire* does not consist merely in the intensity of the desire—as if low-level sex desire for another man's wife is okay and high-level sex desire is not.[15] Nor does the difference reside in whether one remembers choosing to experience the desire—as if choosing to feel sexual desire for another man's wife is sinful while unchosen sexual desire for another man's wife is not. The morally significant difference between sinful lust and harmless desire is neither the *intensity* of the desire nor our own personal sense of its *chosenness*. In biblical literature in general and indeed in Jesus' specific use of the term here, the difference is in the *object* of the desire.[16]

For example, Jesus says that "many prophets and righteous men desired [*epithumeō*] to see what you see, and did not see it" (Matt. 13:17). The word clearly means "desire," and in this case the desire is a good thing because it is a desire to see the messianic kingdom. Likewise, Paul writes that "if any man aspires to the office of overseer, he desires [*epithumeō*] a good work" (1 Tim. 3:1). In both cases, the desire is good because the object of the desire is good. Whether the desire is good (as in Matt. 13:17 or 1 Tim. 3:1) or evil (as in Matt. 5:28) depends entirely on the object that is being desired. That is why this single Greek term is rendered *desire* in some texts and *lust* in others. If you desire something good, then the desire itself is good. If you desire something evil, then the desire itself is evil (i.e., "lustful"). Clearly, having sex with another man's wife is wrong, and so the desire to commit that deed is also wrong. And that is why Jesus prohibits even the desire to commit adultery.

Jesus is not introducing an innovation on this point. It is not as if no one had ever contemplated the moral connection between sinful deeds and the desire that leads to sinful deeds. Again, Jesus is simply connecting the Law's prohibition on adultery in the seventh commandment to the Law's prohibition on the desire for it in the tenth commandment. The term that Jesus uses for *desire* in Matthew 5:28 is taken directly from the Greek version of the tenth commandment, "You shall not *covet* your neighbor's house; you shall not *covet* your neighbor's wife; nor his field, nor his servant, nor his maid, nor his ox, nor his donkey, nor any of his cattle, nor whatever belongs to your neighbor" (Ex. 20:17). What our English translations typically render as *covet* is simply the term for *desire* that we have been looking at in Matthew 5:28—*epithumeō*. Again, our English translations of the tenth commandment render it with a negative connotation ("covet") because the objects of desire are prohibited.[17] Jesus is teaching us that the Ten Commandments—properly understood—prohibit not only adultery and stealing but also the desires that lead to such deeds. The law is not prohibiting *all* desire, but only those desires that have a forbidden object.

Even though Jesus is addressing the issue of adultery in particular in Matthew 5:27–28, he has provided a standard by which we might evaluate sexual desires in general. Indeed, the tenth commandment's prohibition on sinful desire generalizes beyond adultery, and on that basis we are justified to generalize beyond adultery to other forms of illicit desire.[18] And here the implications extend to both heterosexual desire and same-sex desire.

First, the desire that Jesus has in view is specifically sexual desire. Jesus is not talking about desires or attractions that are non-sexual in nature. In other words, we might speak of attractions in some sense that have no sexual possibility embedded within them, but that is simply not what Jesus is talking about here. Jesus is speaking about sex desire specifically. He is talking about the *sexual* attraction that a man might feel for another man's wife.

Second, Jesus invites us to consider the object of the sexual desires and attractions that we experience. In ethical terms, Jesus is teaching us that desire/attraction is teleological. Our desires and attractions tend toward certain ends. If we want to understand our own desires, we have to know what *ends* our desires and attractions are aimed at. We have argued elsewhere that sexual ethics in general are teleological and that the ultimate virtue of our sexual lives consists in glorifying God with our bodies.[19] Here we are arguing essentially the same principle with respect to our desires and attractions. The only sex desire that glorifies God is that desire that is ordered to the covenant of marriage. When sexual desire or attraction fixes on any kind of non-marital erotic activity, it falls short of the glory of God and is, by definition, sinful. Again, this teleological principle applies to every one of our desires, including opposite-sex and same-sex desire. The difference is that opposite-sex desire may have the covenant of marriage as its end or it may not, but same-sex desire can never have the covenant of marriage as its end.

What Makes Jesus' Temptation Innocent?

One common objection to the argument thus far is that this account of things confuses temptation with sinful desire. The objection goes something like this: "The Bible teaches that it is not a sin to be tempted, but you make even the temptation to lust a sin. Are you not saying that all temptation is sin? Wasn't Jesus tempted like us yet without sin (Heb. 4:15)? How can you say that temptation equals sin?"

The short answer to these questions is that we do not believe that all temptation equals sin. Plainly, Jesus was tempted, but he never sinned (Matt. 4:1–11; Heb. 4:15). So unless we want to imply that Jesus was a sinner, we must affirm that not all temptation equals sin. But in saying this, we must be careful to define what we mean by temptation and precisely what our temptation has in common with the temptation that Jesus experienced. Too often we are guilty of projecting our own sinful experiences back onto Jesus. But this is precisely backward. We should not make our sinful experience of temptation the measure of Jesus' sinless experience of temptation. On the contrary, Jesus' sinless experience of temptation should be the measure of ours. There are both similarities and differences between Jesus' experience of temptation and ours.

Yes, Jesus was tempted in every way as we are, but his experience of temptation was not identical to ours. This is the necessary corollary of Christ's sinless perfection—which theologians sometimes call Christ's *impeccability*—and it is anticipated in Hebrews 4:15: "For we do not have a high priest who cannot sympathize with our weaknesses, but One who has been tempted in all things as we are, *yet without sin*" (NASB). There are at least two important observations to make about this text for our purposes.

First, the term for temptation (*peirazō*) in this text is likely a specific reference to the redemptive sufferings of Christ. In general, the verb *peirazō* means *to put someone to the test*.[20] But the only other time Hebrews uses the term in connection with Jesus is in 2:18, which is a specific reference to his sufferings: "For since He Himself was tempted [*peirastheis*] in that which He has suffered, He is able to come to the aid of those who are tempted [*peirazomenois*]" (NASB). Many commentators, therefore, interpret the use of the term in 4:15 in light of its use in 2:18 and conclude that both are a reference to his suffering up to and including the cross.[21] Thus, for Jesus to be tempted in every way as we are does not mean that he himself faced each and every individual trial that each and every human has ever faced. Such an interpretation would of course be absurd. It means that he experienced the ultimate trial and temptation "according to likeness"[22]—a possible allusion to the fact that Jesus suffered as a human. That means that Jesus experienced his sufferings while being subject to all the frailties and weaknesses of embodied life. That is why the New English Bible renders it as "One who, because of his likeness to us, has been tested every way, only without sin."[23]

Second, the key thing to note about Jesus' suffering and temptation is that it was "without sin." There was no aspect of Jesus' temptation that ever involved sin on his part. He had no desires that predisposed him to sin. His response to external pressures never resulted in an evil thought or attraction. And, of course, he never engaged in any sinful response to the suffering that he faced. From top to bottom, he was perfect, innocent, wholesome, and good in the face of every temptation. That means that Jesus' experience of temptation was never internalized into any disposition toward evil. Ever. Jesus' attractions—whatever they were—were never directed toward something that his Father had prohibited. Jesus' impeccability means not merely that he never sinned but that it was not possible for him to sin.[24] Thus we agree with Augustine, "God forbid that we should ever say that He is able to sin!"[25]

This is not our experience of temptation. We experience a level of internalization that Jesus' impeccability never allowed. Yes, he faced the same sorts of external pressures to sin. No, those pressures never had a landing pad in his heart. In the face of withering satanic attacks, he only always desired his Father's will (Matt. 26:39; John 5:19). The words "without sin" indicate that, while Jesus faced temptations as we do, his experience of those temptations was quite different from ours in that his was *always* sinless.

Jesus' impeccability in this regard has provoked some people to wonder whether his experience of temptation can ever be as intense as that of the sinners that he came to save. Can he really have known our weaknesses when he himself was not capable of sinning? This question points us to a glorious irony of Jesus' sinless nature. It did not lessen his experience of temptation but only intensified it. Leon Morris has said it this way:

> The man who yields to a particular temptation has not yet felt its full power. He has given in while the temptation has yet something in reserve. Only the man who does not yield to a temptation[,] who, as regards that particular temptation, is sinless, knows the full extent of that temptation.[26]

What Makes Our Temptation Sinful?

All temptation has at least two defining elements—a trial and an enticement to sin. The trial is an experience of testing that often includes suffering or a sense of deprivation. The enticement consists of an allurement to relieve suffering or deprivation through sin. When Satan tempted Jesus in the wilderness, both elements were present. Jesus' hunger was a trial that made him experience physical hunger. Satan offers Jesus bread in order to entice Jesus to relieve that condition through sinful means.[27] Although trial and enticement can be distinguished conceptually, they cannot always be separated experientially. Sometimes the trial *is* the enticement to sin. Sometimes the trial *leads* to the enticement to sin. In either case, temptation always includes both elements— trial and enticement.

One distinguishing mark of Jesus' experience of temptation is that the *enticement* to sin never emerged from his own nature. He was sinless. He had no sin nature. There was nothing in his sinless nature that could have produced a desire for evil. Jesus could experience trials in the same way that sinners do. But he never experienced *enticement* to evil emerging from his own nature. Sinners, however, often experience enticement to evil that originates in their own sinful nature. This is exactly how James describes our experience in James 1:13–15.

> Let no one say when he is tempted, "I am being tempted by God"; for God cannot be tempted by evil, and He Himself does not tempt anyone. But each one is tempted when he is carried away and enticed *by his own desire* [*epithumias*]. Then when desire has conceived, it gives birth to sin; and when sin is accomplished, it brings forth death.

The temptation in "each one is tempted" is explicitly tied to the sinner's inner inclination. Literally, "each one is tempted when, *by his own desire*, he is carried away and enticed." In this context, the desire is not an issue of moral indifference. The word translated as "desire" (ESV) or "lust" (NASB) is *epithumia*. Again, the only time *epithumia* is good is when it is directed toward something morally praiseworthy. *Epithumia* is always evil when it is directed toward something morally blameworthy. Thus, "desire" is not neutral anywhere in this text. It is a "desire" that "lures" and "entices." In short, it is a desire that is directed toward evil. Thus the desire itself is sinful. When such illicit desire conceives, it inevitably gives birth to sin because it *is* sin. As Doug Moo contends, "James now attributes temptation to each person's *evil desire* . . . [defined as] any human longing for what God has prohibited."[28]

The text also says that God cannot be tempted by evil but that sinners obviously are. In what way are we tempted by evil that God is not tempted by evil? Verse 14 gives the answer. We face temptations that arise from our "own desire" (1:14). In contrast, Jesus never faced temptations arising from "his own sinful desire." As God, he could not and cannot be tempted by evil in this way. His heart never in any degree fixated on evil. Temptation had no landing pad in Jesus' heart and neither did it have a launching pad from Jesus' heart. The same is not true of sinners, who are often carried away by their own desires, as James describes it.

We can speak of two different ways of experiencing temptation. On the one hand, there is temptation that comes to us from the outside. Jesus' temptations in the wilderness were of this sort. The *enticement* to sin came from Satan, not from Jesus' nature. On the other hand, there is temptation that comes to us from the inside. In this case, the *enticement* to sin comes from our own sinful desires. The sinner's temptations are often of this sort. In his comments on James 1:13–15, John Owen explains,

> Now, when such a temptation comes from without, it is unto the soul an indifferent thing, neither good nor evil, unless it be consented unto; but the very proposal from *within*, it being the soul's own act, is its sin.[29]

Temptation is not sinful when it comes at us from the outside. In the wilderness temptation, the enticement to sin came from Satan, not from Jesus. And that is why Jesus was able to be tempted and yet be without sin (Heb. 4:15). But when the enticement to sin emerges from our own sinful nature, that is an entirely different matter. In that case, the temptation *itself* is sinful. That is an experience that is unique to sinners and that Jesus himself never experienced.

There is another way in which our temptation differs from that of Jesus. When a sinner gives in to temptation, the transgression creates new temptations that may themselves be sinful. For example, because we often give in to the sin of covetousness, we are tempted by our own covetousness to get angry at anyone who deprives us of what we want. In that situation, the temptation to anger is our own covetousness. So the temptation is already sinful, and it is providing an occasion for another sin (anger) to emerge. Our sin snowballs, and one sin becomes a temptation for another sin. This never happened with Jesus. Jesus is not tempted by evil in this way. Because he never sinned, he never experienced the snowball effect that we experience. The one who gives in to temptation soon learns that sin does not satisfy sinful desires. It awakens them. And this never happened inside Jesus, but it happens to sinners continuously.

So it is possible to be tempted and not to sin. One can experience a trial and yet feel no desire to relieve that trial through sinful means. Jesus faced such temptations and never sinned, either in desire or in deed. Sinners can experience trials in the same way and yet not sin. But when sinners are tempted to do evil by their own fallen desires, the temptation itself is sinful.

But what about the progression of thought that James describes? How can we claim that the desire *is* sin when James seems to say only that desire *leads* to sin?[30] The answer to these questions is found in the different ways that the New Testament uses the word "sin" (*hamartia*). The Bible uses the term *sin* in at least two distinct senses. In some texts, it's a reference to sinful deeds (e.g., 1 Tim. 5:24). In other texts, *sin* refers to a sinful principle/inclination that resides in the human heart (e.g., Rom. 7:20, 23).[31] James uses the word seven times in his letter, and every other appearance of the term clearly refers to sinful deeds (see James 1:15; 2:9; 4:17; 5:15, 16, 20). That is what *sin* refers to in James 1:15 as well. So James' point is a simple one. Fallen desire gives birth to sinful deeds. But it is a non sequitur to conclude that James' reference to "desire" has no moral dimension to it. James is clear that the desire that leads to the sinful deed is indeed fallen. The desire "lures" and "entices" the sinner away from faithfulness and to sin. Even though James doesn't use the word *sin* to refer to such desire, the apostle Paul does. Romans 7 is a chapter-long meditation on sinful desire (*epithumia*), and Paul unambiguously labels it as *sin* (see Rom. 7:20, 23). We are on firm ground to regard it as such in James 1 as well. In his commentary on James 1, Sam Allberry explains it this way:

> The uncomfortable truth is this: the evil desire tugging away at us *is our own*. We can't blame any of the things around us. It is not the fault of our parents, our peers, our circumstances, our genes or our God. . . . My circumstances may be the occasion for my sin, but they are not the cause of it.
>
> No, our own desires are the cause of temptation. The desire to sin that wells up within us comes from our own hearts. Temptation would not be tempting if I were pure and not evil. This is reinforced by what James tells us about how temptation works. . . .
>
> James is showing us something deeply profound about our human nature, for we are both agent and victim of our desires. The desires are our own, from our own hearts—yet it is us that they entice and attack. Within each of us there is this deep tension. We really are our own worst enemies.[32]

A crucial distinction between our experience and Jesus' experience is that we often face temptation arising from our own fallen desire. Moreover, we move rather seamlessly and unconsciously from experience of trial to desire for evil. Jesus' experience of temptation never happened that way. He experienced trials just as we do, yet he was always without sin.

What Jesus Teaches Us about the "Way of Escape"

If all of this is true, then what does it mean for us to be tempted while not sinning? After all, the apostle Paul says that God always provides "the way of escape" for us when we are tempted (1 Cor. 10:13).

Our experience of temptation can possibly have both external and internal aspects. Jesus faced external "testing" just like we do. Satan set before Jesus "temptations," but those temptations never emerged from his own desires. Nor did he ever experience the sin snowball as we do. Satan never laid a finger on Jesus' holy resolve to do all his Father's holy will. Jesus experienced "temptation" in that external sense, but the temptations never had a place within his heart. Biblically speaking, that is the moral space between temptation and sin. As long as temptation does not emerge from one's own sinful desire, the mere experience of the temptation is not sinful. But sin is conceived when desire fixes on evil.

Consider how this pattern plays out in our own experience of sexual temptation. Perhaps Satan would set before a man an image of an attractive married woman. He might see her and apprehend that she is beautiful. But the moment that apprehension turns into a sexual attraction for her, it is sin within his heart. It has moved from an external temptation to an internal attraction that is unwholesome and forbidden by Scripture. Sinners leap right over this moral space all the time. It is so easy and natural to us. But Jesus never did. Such temptations were wholly external to his desires—he never desired something that his Father had forbidden.

This aspect of Jesus' impeccability ought to evoke worship when we really think about it. Jesus always looked at every woman and every man in a way that was without sin. He never experienced an untoward sexual desire for any person. He was able to sit with the woman at the well, for example, without the turmoil of disordered lusts that he ought not to be feeling (John 4:1–42). When the disciples asked Jesus if he was hungry, Jesus said this about his interaction with the Samaritan woman: "My food is to do the will of Him who sent Me, and to accomplish His work" (John 4:34 NASB). No physical urge ever trumped his desire to do his Father's will. He just saw her, loved her, and ministered to her without the sinful wrestlings that we have to reckon with. Maybe she was beautiful. Maybe there was a bait to lust there. She had already made herself sexually available to at least five different men. And he was alone with her. But there was no place for that temptation to land in Jesus' heart. He was perfect. He always got it right both in his heart and in his deeds.

We err if we project our own sinful experience of temptation onto Jesus. Sometimes the desire for evil emerges from our own sinful nature. Because he had no sin nature, Jesus never experienced this kind of temptation. We often respond to external temptation with a desire for evil. Jesus never responded to temptation like that. Sometimes our giving in to temptation snowballs into other temptations. This never happened to Jesus either. He was completely sinless. Is temptation the same thing as sin? No, not necessarily. But let us not think that our frequent attraction to evil ever had a parallel in Jesus' heart. It did not.

Discerning the Truth about Same-Sex Attraction

So how does all this talk of temptation, desire, and sin map onto the contemporary notion of sexual orientation? And, in particular, does it help us at all to answer the question we posed at the outset: "Is same-sex attraction sinful?" In the previous chapter, we identified three components of sexual orientation—sexual attraction, emotional attraction, and identity (with sexual attraction being the defining feature). Insofar as same-sex orientation designates the experience of sexual desire for a person of the same sex, yes, it is sinful. Insofar as same-sex orientation indicates emotional/romantic attractions that brim with erotic possibility, yes, those attractions, too, are sinful. Insofar as sexual orientation designates an identity, yes, that identity, too, is a sinful fiction that contradicts God's purposes for his creation.

If these observations about sexual orientation are true, there are numerous pastoral implications. We will mention just three.

First, to call same-sex orientation sinful does not make same-sex–attracted people less like the rest of us. On the contrary, it makes them more like the rest of us. We are not singling out same-sex–attracted people as if their experience is somehow more repugnant than everyone else's experience of living with a sinful nature. All of us bear the marks of our connection to Adam. All of us are crooked deep down. All of us have thoughts, inclinations, attitudes, and the like that are deeply antithetical to God's law. All of us need a renewal from the inside out that can come only from the grace of Christ. We are in this predicament together. We do not stand apart.

Second, these truths ought to inform how brothers and sisters in Christ wage war against same-sex attraction. Sin is not merely what we do. It is also who we are. As so many of our confessions have it, we are sinners by nature and by choice.[33] All of us are born with an orientation toward sin. The ongoing experience of same-sex sexual attraction is but one manifestation of our common experience of indwelling sin—indeed of the mind set on the flesh (Rom. 7:23; 8:7). For that reason, the Bible teaches us to war against both the root and the fruit of sin. In this case, same-sex attraction is the root, and same-sex sexual behavior is the fruit. The Spirit of God aims to transform both (Rom. 8:13).

If same-sex attraction were morally benign, there would be no reason to repent of it. But the Bible never treats sexual attraction to the same sex as a morally neutral state. Jesus says all sexual immorality is fundamentally a matter of the heart. Thus it will not do simply to avoid same-sex behavior. The ordinary means of grace must be aimed at the heart as well. Prayer, the preaching of the Word, and the fellowship of the saints must all be aimed at the Holy Spirit's renewal of the inner man (2 Cor. 4:16). It is to be a spiritual transformation that puts to death the deeds of the body by a daily renewal of the mind (Rom. 8:13; 12:2). The aim of this transformation is not heterosexuality but holiness.[34]

This is not to say that Christians who experience same-sex attraction will necessarily be freed from those desires completely in this life. Many such Christians report partial or complete changes in their attractions after conversion—sometimes all at once, but more often over a period of months and years. But those cases are not the norm. There are a great many who also report ongoing struggles with same-sex attraction.[35] But that does not lessen the responsibility for them to fight those desires as long as they persist, no matter how natural those desires may feel. The Bible teaches that the Holy Spirit can bring about this kind of transformation in anyone—even if such progress is not experienced by everyone in precisely the same measure. As the apostle Paul writes, "Thanks be to God that though you were slaves of sin, you became obedient from the heart to that form of teaching to which you were committed" (Rom. 6:17 NASB).

Third, this truth ought to strengthen our love and compassion for brothers and sisters who experience same-sex attraction. For many of them, same-sex attraction is something they have experienced for as long as they can remember. There is no obvious pathology for their attractions. The attractions are what they are, even though they may be quite unwelcome. It is naive to think that these people are all outside the church. No, they are among us. They are us. They have been baptized, have been attending the Lord's Table with us, and have been fighting the good fight in what is sometimes a very lonely struggle. They believe what the Bible says about their sexuality, but their struggle is nevertheless difficult.

Is your church the kind of place that would be safe for these dear brothers and sisters to come forward and find friendship and community? Is your home the kind of place that would be safe for these dear brothers and sisters to come forward and find friendship and community? Do your church and your home have arms wide open to them to come alongside them, to receive them, and to strengthen them? Jesus said that the world would know us by our love for one another (John 13:35). One of the ways that we show love for one another is by bearing one another's burdens (Gal. 6:2). Can you bear this burden with your brothers and sisters who are in this fight? Are you ready to offer help and encouragement to these saints for whom Christ died? If not, then something is deeply amiss. For Jesus has loved us to the uttermost, and he calls us to do the same (John 13:34).

Questions for Reflection

1. Does Augustine believe that the desire for sexual sin is sin? How does his view differ from the Roman Catholic position?

2. Why is neither the intensity of a sinful desire nor one's own sense of personal choice for the desire an adequate standard to use when distinguishing desires as sinful or not?

3. In what way or ways are Christ's temptations like ours? In what way or ways are his experience of temptation different from ours?

4. How can the concluding pastoral implications of this chapter impact your own ministry to those who struggle with same-sex attraction?

PART TWO

The Path of Transformation

3

Myths about Change

When we come to the topic of change, we arrive at something very controversial. The secular wisdom of our culture is that change regarding homosexuality is not only impossible, but also harmful. We are constantly advised that the pursuit of change is a relic and should be disregarded for the good of those with same-sex attraction.

As biblical Christians, we must take strong exception to this. We must confess that change is possible for any problem. We must be clear that if God gives clear commands, he will, over time and by his grace, give the strength to obey those commands. As we turn our thoughts to the issue of the possibility of change, we will discuss it in two parts.

In the next chapter we will talk about what biblical change truly is and how to pursue it. In this chapter we will discuss what biblical change is *not*. Because the topic of change concerning same-sex attraction is so controversial, we must be very clear what we are not talking about. In order to unpack what biblical change is not we will explore five popular myths about change regarding same-sex attraction.

Myth #1: An Understanding of Biblical Ethics Leads to Biblical Change

So far in this book we have been talking about ethics. We have been trying to argue that it is homosexual behavior as well as homosexual desires—sometimes understood as orientation—that are sinful.

As we stated in the beginning of this book, an understanding of ethics is crucial. It has to do with the issue of which behaviors are right and wrong. Without an understanding of biblical ethics, it would be impossible to know which desires and actions are acceptable or unacceptable. As important as ethics are, however, they do not change people. Knowing that a particular behavior is wrong does not give someone the resources and ability to do what is right. That means that, as important as it is to have a discussion about ethics, this only comprises the beginning of the Christian responsibility on this matter. As Christians, we cannot only talk about ethics. We must also discuss ministry.

Ministry is inseparable from ethics. Ministry has to do with coming alongside hurting and troubled people and using biblical resources to help them conform their lives to biblical standards. Ministry is hard work because, in addition to understanding ethical principles, you need to understand people. Understanding people requires a listening ear, a sensitive and humble heart, and a firm resolve to walk side by side with others, offering help over the long haul.

It is crucial for us to make the transition from ethics to ministry on the topic of same-sex attraction. The truth is that well-meaning Christians have added to the burden that many same-sex–attracted people carry. We do this whenever we are crystal clear about the sinfulness of homosexuality without being clear about how to change.[1] If you or someone you know has struggled with homosexual desires, you have likely felt this frustration. You want to change. You have tried to change. You agree with Christians that you need to change. You have discovered, however, how difficult it can be to change.

Almost everyone who struggles with same-sex attraction experiences how hard it is to walk the journey of change. Temptation is constant. Failure abounds. Frustration clouds the mind. Christians experiencing same-sex attraction want to know why it is so hard to change when God's Word is so clear. They want to know how change could be so elusive when they are fervent in their desire to honor Christ. One reason that change is so hard to achieve is that Christians have excelled in ethics while overlooking ministry. In this book, we want to plead with faithful Christians to add a robust understanding of ministry to their profound articulation of sexual ethics. If we get the ethics right without growing in our ability to do ministry, we will fail the many struggling people who are desperate for transformation.

Myth #2: Change Is Impossible

Many today argue that homosexual desires cannot be changed. This argument is the premise of the book by Matthew Vines that we mentioned earlier. Vines says,

> For years, many conservative Christians supported efforts to change gay people's sexual orientation. Some still take that approach, but in 2013, the flagship "ex-gay" organization shut down after acknowledging that it is futile—and often harmful—to attempt to change people's sexual orientation. The failure of that movement has left evangelicals grappling with how to respond to the reality of sexual orientation without compromising their beliefs.[2]

Vines believes that it is "futile" to attempt to change one's sexual desires. He bases his argument for this futility on the closure of an umbrella organization that united several different ex-gay ministries. He also bases it on personal stories that he relates throughout his book—stories of people who were unsuccessful in their efforts at change.

Vines is making an important point that must not be overlooked. He concentrates on the difficulty of change and the profound sense of pain that attends that difficulty. Vines, those he knows, and many who sought help from the Exodus International ministry have an experience to report that we need to hear. The experience is one of tremendous difficulty in trying to change their sexual orientation. These people have experienced profound anguish as they have done everything they know to do to be freed from a problem that they did not want and do not know how to change.

As essential as it is to understand the experiences of people in such turmoil, it is important to note that Vines's argument arrives at a premature conclusion. He takes the collapse of Exodus and the stories of failed change as the evidence that same-sex attraction cannot be changed. This conclusion is illegitimate. In strictly logical terms it is a possibility, but it is only *one* possibility. Exodus International certainly did close, and there are many people to whom Vines (and the rest of us!) could point who have experienced a difficult road to change. But those facts do not necessarily mean that change is *impossible*.

No one disputes that change is hard. There are, however, all sorts of reasons why a person who struggles with same-sex attraction might experience difficulty changing. Perhaps it *is* impossible to change. Other explanations are available, however. Change may be elusive because growing cultural acceptance of homosexuality discourages it. Perhaps some who have tried to change have not been truly committed to the process. It may be that change is a long, hard road that takes a long time. It also may be the case that some have not yet figured out the correct way to help people change. Any one of these explanations, as well as some combinations of them, could explain the difficulty that many people experience.

It is interesting, however, that of all these options, Vines assumes the only one that is demonstrably untrue. The first place we need to go to see that it is untrue is in the timelessly authoritative teachings of Scripture.

Scripture

The Bible is clear about homosexuality. Every single reference to homosexual behavior in the Bible is a negative reference. The only sexual behavior ever endorsed by Scripture is the kind that happens between one man and one woman in the context of marriage. There is no exception to this biblical ethic. The Bible, though, does not just talk about *ethics*. The Bible also talks about *ministry*. In particular, every page of the New Testament talks about how Jesus Christ changes and purifies us by his grace.

One place where the Bible teaches this is Romans 8:9–11.

> You, however, are not in the flesh but in the Spirit, if in fact the Spirit of God dwells in you. Anyone who does not have the Spirit of Christ does not belong to him. But if Christ is in you, although the body is dead because of sin, the Spirit is life because of righteousness. If the Spirit of him who raised Jesus from the dead dwells in you, he who raised Christ Jesus from the dead will also give life to your mortal bodies through the Spirit who dwells in you.

Paul provides an amazing demonstration of God's grace in Christ. Follow us through three observations about this text.

The first observation is that Jesus Christ was dead. He had no pulse. His bones were frozen with rigor mortis. His organs were cold and still. As pastors, we have been in the room with many sick people and have watched them take their last breath as they lost a fight with a terminal diagnosis. We have officiated at scores of funerals. We have seen many people weep over the bodies of their dead loved ones, pleading for them to come back.

In those difficult experiences we have learned a very painful and fundamental lesson: death is final. There is no human way to turn it back. In spite of the best medical skill and technology, humanity has no way to restore a spirit torn from its body. In human terms, death is truly the end of the line.

Jesus was just as dead as any person we have ever stood over while preaching a funeral sermon. His life was over. The situation appeared hopeless.

That leads to the second observation. Jesus Christ was restored to life, in spite of the apparent hopelessness of his situation. God did, in the physical body of Jesus, what is impossible for anyone else. He restored to life a person who had been dead for three days. We must be careful with this truth. If we are not cautious, we will grow too familiar with this mind-blowing reality! We should never let our acquaintance with it cause our jaws to fail to drop. How could God do something so apparently impossible? What power was available to God that would allow him to perform such a miracle? In Romans 8:11 Paul gives us the answer. He tells us that Jesus was raised to life by the power of the Holy Spirit.

This reality gets us to the third observation. Paul tells us that the same Spirit who raised Jesus to life is the one who dwells in believers. It is that same powerful Spirit who gives life to the mortal bodies of Christians as they put off sin and put on righteousness. This truth is truly overwhelming. The same power that Jesus had to be restored to life is the same power that Christians have for moral change. If you are a believer in Jesus Christ, you have the Spirit of Christ dwelling in you to empower your change in any moral category. This is just as true for same-sex attraction as it is for any other sin.

When discussing the necessity and power for change, many Christians point to 1 Corinthians 6:9–11. That passage lists homosexuality as one of the sins that block people from the kingdom of God. It further confirms that Christians are no longer defined by that sin but have been washed, sanctified, and justified by the Spirit. We love that passage, believe it is crucial to this topic, and have even unpacked it in other writings.[3]

The point in focusing on a different passage in this space is to highlight the fact that 1 Corinthians 6 is not the only passage in the New Testament that addresses this issue. The Bible is full of teaching on the resources available to Christians to provide power for change. In fact, this is one way to describe the subject matter of the entire Bible. It is written to show us how to overcome sin by the power of Jesus Christ.

Paul's teaching in Romans 8 is particularly relevant in light of his teaching in Romans 1. In that vitally important chapter, Paul makes clear that God's wrath is revealed in his giving up of people to homosexual sin. It is a truly devastating picture of the carnage of sin in a sinful world. We need to remember, however, that Paul is merely beginning an argument in the introductory chapter of Romans. We should not stop reading at Romans 1, and neither should we forget that chapter when we get to the hope-filled content of Romans 8. Paul intends the powerful teaching of Romans 8 to dispel the discouragement of Romans 1. The same Spirit that overwhelmed Jesus' corpse with life is able powerfully to change those with sexual desires like those described in Romans 1. If 1 Corinthians had never been written, Romans 1–8 would be enough to convince us that profound change is just as possible for homosexual sin as it is for any other.

Stories

There is another place we can go to demonstrate that change is possible. It is the many stories of people who have experienced change in their sexual desires. You may have heard of the

Christian musician Dennis Jernigan. He is the composer of many popular songs like "We Will Worship the Lamb of Glory" and "You are My All in All." What you may not know is that Jernigan grew up with a same-sex attraction. He recounts his story in the powerful documentary *Sing Over Me*.[4]

Jernigan relates the profound pain he experienced as he lived with same-sex attraction. He also describes the carnage of living a promiscuously gay lifestyle. What makes the documentary so encouraging, however, is the powerful testimony of change that attended his conversion to faith in the Lord Jesus. Jernigan was exclusively same-sex attracted, but since he became a Christian, all that has changed. Jernigan has been married to the same woman for over thirty years and is the father of nine children.

This is just one story. We could share many more. We are personally familiar with many men who were once defined by homosexual lust but are not any longer. There are many men and women with more public profiles who report change—people like Anne Paulk, Christopher Yuan, Sam Allberry, Nick Roen and more. Not all of these people have the same stories of change to tell. Some have pursued different methods of change than others. Some are married; others are single. All of them, however, are seeking to honor Jesus with their sexuality. All of them are different than they were when they first believed.

These stories are important. Many people recount the stories of those who have tried to change and have failed. We believe those stories and admit that change is hard. Listening is a two-way street, however. It is just as unkind and unloving to ignore the stories of those who have found it impossible to change as it is to ignore the stories of those who have found it possible to change. And those stories are out there for those who are willing to hear them.[5] We need to listen to everyone. You do not have to discount someone else's testimony to make yours valuable.

When you listen to everyone, you will find that change is hard. It is so hard that, to many, it *feels* impossible. What Scripture and the stories of many tell us, though, is that change is possible. This is not to say that anyone will experience moral perfection in this life. Change is a process that involves progress over time, and it does not necessarily occur at the same rate or in the same measure in every person. Nevertheless, it can be done because it has been done, and the Bible promises that it can be done. The most common explanation for the difficulty of change in our culture is that change is impossible. Too many people have changed for this to be true, however. Even more than that, God's inspired Word disproves the claim. It is, therefore, a myth that change is impossible.

Myth #3: Change Is Harmful

Another myth that is repeated very often is that change is harmful to those struggling with homosexuality—even to the point of being deadly. In 2012, the state of California passed a law banning a type of therapy referred to as conversion or reparative therapy. The bill was sponsored by state senator Ted Lieu, who explained the rationale for the law in candid terms, "An entire house of medicine has rejected gay conversion therapy. Not only does it not work, but it is harmful. Patients who go through this have gone through guilt and shame, and some have committed suicide."[6]

Sen. Lieu articulates a sentiment that is frequently repeated: efforts to change homosexual desires are personally harmful to the point of suicide. There is so much support for this belief that a bill was passed into law—a law whose sole purpose was to protect people from the supposed dangers of attempts at change. The state of New Jersey has since passed its own law, and other states are considering similar measures. Even the White House has issued a statement denouncing "any practices by mental health providers that seek to change an individual's sexual orientation or gender identity."[7]

Reparative therapy proposes significant problems for Christians who want to minister to people struggling with same-sex attraction. We will interact with some of these problems below.[8] It is one thing to say that there are problems with reparative therapy; it is another thing to say that it is *deadly* to try to help people who are struggling with homosexuality to change. Many homosexual men and women do make many tragic efforts to end their lives. It is an unwarranted assumption, however, that people resort to self-harm and suicide because of efforts to help them change. This assumption overlooks the obvious fact that homosexuality is dangerous on its own well before anyone says it is wrong or intervenes in someone's life to help bring about change.

Homosexuality is dangerous. *The Journal of the American Medical Association* reports that male homosexuals experience a 4,000 percent higher risk of anal cancer than the rest of the population.[9] Male homosexuals with a long-term partner live, on average, thirty years shorter than heterosexual men.[10] These and other factors are why homosexual men are at such high risk for emotional and spiritual problems. This was the conclusion of J. Michael Bailey concerning several studies on homosexuality:

> These studies contain arguably the best published data on the association between homosexuality and psychopathology, and both converge on the same unhappy conclusion: homosexual people are at substantially higher risk for some forms of emotional problems, including suicidality, major depression, and anxiety disorder, [and] conduct disorder.[11]

When anyone enters into the work of helping a homosexual to change, a dangerous task is being undertaken. The danger is intrinsic not to the work of change, however, but to the deeply troubled people fighting against a serious problem. When a patient dies in a hospital trauma ward, we do not blame the attempt at care, but understand the inherent difficulty of the work, and we seek advances toward improved treatment. We should think the same way about people struggling with homosexuality. The difficulties experienced by those who struggle underline the demand that exists for all of us—but especially Christians—to grow in our ability to administer effective pastoral care.

Myth #4: Change Requires Heterosexual Desire

One of the most painful and persistent myths about this issue has to do with the goal of change. Many are confused, believing that the goal of change is heterosexuality. The confusion is captured well by Justin Lee in his book *Torn: Rescuing the Gospel from the Gays-Vs.-Christians Debate*. He relates a heart-wrenching account of his struggle to change his homosexual orientation. One such attempt led him to meet with a group of men in his church who likewise struggled with same-sex attraction. In his account, he shares an event that was particularly discouraging to him.

At one point in the meeting, a tired-looking man with a wedding ring on his finger said that he had some exiting news to share. Everyone leaned forward.

"This weekend," he said, "my wife and kids and I took a trip to the beach. While we were there, a woman walked by in a small bikini. And I *noticed* her."

He sat back with a satisfied smile. The small group erupted in cheers and congratulations. Clearly, for him this was a milestone achievement—noticing a woman on the beach.

> I sat transfixed and horrified. Was this to be my destiny?
> What kind of life would that be? . . . I wanted more than that
> for my life. . . . I wanted to have to struggle to avoid lusting
> after women. . . . This wasn't the kind of future I wanted. I
> wanted to change my feelings, not just get married in spite of
> them. I wasn't going to be like these guys. I was going to be
> completely straight.[12]

Notice how Lee and the men he describes equate change with being "completely straight." He even expresses an ironic desire to trade homosexual lust for heterosexual lust. Lee and those who he describes had decided that the goal of change was heterosexuality. They felt understandable pain and brokenness when that goal proved repeatedly to be elusive.

The problem is that they learned about this goal not from the Bible but from secular reparative therapy. Though much of reparative therapy is built on an unbiblical foundation, its teachings have unfortunately been embraced by many Christians who are eager to help people change. Moreover, many non-Christians mistakenly think that the teachings of reparative therapy represent the Christian approach to change. Reparative therapists believe that the goal of change is heterosexuality. The leading proponent of reparative therapy, Joseph Nicolosi, makes this clear. "As shame is slowly diminished in therapy and the same-sex attracted man grows in self-awareness and self-assertion, he should gradually begin to find within himself a natural heterosexual response."[13] Based on teachings like this, many Christians have been led to undue frustration and despair. The Bible, on the other hand, provides a much more helpful goal.

In Scripture, same-sex attraction and behavior are repeatedly and consistently condemned. Because of that reality, it is possible to wrongly assume that opposite-sex attraction and behavior are repeatedly endorsed. In fact, this is not the case. The Bible never portrays heterosexuality in general to be a good thing. There is not one place in the entire Bible where men and women are commanded to have sexual desire for the opposite sex indiscriminately. The biblical norm for our sexual lives is chastity outside of marriage and fidelity within marriage. Thus the marriage covenant provides the norm for our sexual lives, not heterosexuality as an identity category.

What the Bible does command is sexual desire for one's spouse. One place where this is clear is in Proverbs 5:18–19:

> Let your fountain be blessed,
>> and rejoice in the wife of your youth,
>> a lovely deer, a graceful doe.
> Let her breasts fill you at all times with delight;
>> be intoxicated always in her love.

This passage is crystal clear—even explicit—about the sexual desire that should attend a man's relationship with his wife. The sexual desire that is commanded in this passage—as in every biblical example—is directed not to women in general but to one's wife in particular. In the Bible, men and women are to have sexual desire for their spouse, not for the opposite sex in general.

What the Bible commands, therefore, is not heterosexuality but holiness. Christians are called to pursue purity. In biblical terms this means that Christians are called to mortify every sexual desire that is not directed toward one's spouse in biblical marriage. This creates a wonderful amount of freedom for those struggling with homosexual attraction. They no longer have to pursue being "straight" as the only goal. They can, instead, pursue the biblical goal of purity. They have two options to do this.

Many who struggle with homosexual desire will have a good and appropriate desire for the kind of care and companionship that attends marriage. They will be aware of desires for the kind of relational care, family, accountability, and—yes—sexual expression that comes exclusively in Christian marriage. As we noted above, there are many people who have successfully pursued this goal. Their stories are true and powerful even though it is often politically incorrect to share them.

Others will not experience this desire. They will be aware of a total lack of desire for the kind of opposite-sex companionship that is part and parcel of marriage. They may be aware of a total lack of physical desire to fulfill the sexual obligations required in marriage (1 Cor. 7:1–5). Such people have the biblical option of pursuing the high calling of Christian singleness and celibacy (Matt. 19:10–12; 1 Cor. 7:25–38).

The biblical goal of purity, in its manifestations of marriage for some and celibacy for others, replaces the unbiblical goal of heterosexual desire for all people. As this purity is pursued, there are two things to keep in mind. First, only the goals taught in Scripture will receive the power of the Holy Spirit to accomplish them. One of the reasons that some people have experienced frustration and failure in their attempts at change is that they have been pursuing a goal for which the Holy Spirit of God has not been supplying grace. The Holy Spirit will not supply grace to pursue a goal he has not commanded. The Spirit is not interested in empowering heterosexual lust any more than the homosexual variety.

Second, as the Spirit empowers us to pursue these goals, we should not expect that our pursuit of them will be perfect. It is no more scandalous for a person pursuing celibacy or marriage to battle homosexual lust than it is for that person to battle heterosexual lust. All of us are growing in our ability to lay hold of Christ and to mortify sinful, sexual desires. Those of us who battle heterosexual lust need Jesus' grace as much as our friends and brothers do who struggle with same-sex attraction. We would not say that a person who is fighting against ongoing temptation to look at pornography has not changed or can never change because of the presence of a current struggle. We would give thanks for all the ways in which such a person has changed and would help him grow in his ability to fight effectively. The same is true for those who battle same-sex attraction. This means that it is not only a myth to claim that change requires heterosexuality. It is also a myth to claim that change requires a perfect purifying of our desires this side of heaven.

Myth #5: Change Happens without Repentance

As we conclude this chapter on myths about change, we have established a lot of helpful realities. We have established that change requires more than an understanding of ethics, that it is possible, that it is not harmful, and that it does not require heterosexuality to be complete. There is one crucial reality, however, yet to be addressed. That one reality concerns how people actually pursue change. If change is a reality that is good for struggling people, then how do they pursue it? Many important steps on the path to change will be discussed in the next chapter. As we conclude this chapter, it is not as important for us to focus on the *steps* as it is to focus on the *path* itself. In the Bible, the path of change is the path of repentance.

This understanding is crucial because so many approaches to change attempt to use a path other than repentance. With regard to homosexuality, the most popular alternate path Christians have embraced has been reparative therapy.

Reparative therapy marginalizes repentance by embracing a faulty understanding of what causes homosexuality and by pursuing a faulty process of change. Reparative therapists believe that homosexuality is caused by broken relationships between parents and their young, "pre-homosexual" children. When children, especially boys, experience a break in the relationship with their parent of the same sex, they fail to develop appropriate same-sex attachments. This loss of attachment leads to a desire, later in life, to repair this attachment through homosexual sex.[14]

The problem here is that the Bible rather obviously locates the problem of homosexuality in sin, not in broken parental attachments. Significant numbers of homosexual men do report difficult relationships with their fathers. There are, however, plenty of homosexual men who have great relationships with their dads. There are also large numbers of men who have terrible relationships with their fathers but are not gay. The explanation for homosexuality from reparative therapy does not work because it ignores all this other data. More importantly, it fails to call homosexuality a sin before the living God. Reparative therapists believe that homosexuality is dangerous and at odds with human thriving. That is true, but it is not enough. We must also say that homosexuality is more than maladaptive. It is a sin against the living God. Failing to affirm this central truth undercuts repentance because there is no need for repentance where there is no sin.

Reparative therapy also marginalizes repentance by pursuing a faulty process of change. The goal of reparative therapy is to repair the loss of parental attachment through the therapeutic relationship. The reparative therapist engages in a loving, affirming, and non-sexual relationship with his client in order to develop the kind of confidence and assertiveness that was not created in childhood.[15] This poses a massive problem from a biblical perspective. The Bible does not teach that sin is changed through some kind of therapeutic re-parenting. The Bible teaches that change happens as believers lay hold of the grace of the Lord Jesus Christ through repentance, and as they confess their sin, pleading with God for his grace to change them.

The chief problem with reparative therapy is not that those who practice it have no success stories, still less that it is cruel in some way. The problem with it is that it obscures the glory of Jesus Christ by refusing to label homosexuality as sin. This tragic failure discourages people from calling out to the Savior who, through his atoning grace alone, can free them from such a powerful struggle.

There is one other thing we must address concerning this myth. Not only is repentance the only path to change, but *deep* repentance is the only path to change. That is to say that change requires more than repentance at the level of behavior. It also requires repentance at the level of the desires that produce those behaviors.

One of the most revolutionary teachings in the Bible about our behavior is that our actions always spring from the desires of our heart. Solomon reflects this belief when he instructs that we should guard our hearts because everything else in our lives flows from them (Proverbs 4:23). Jesus teaches this when he explains that all of our behaviors, like sexual immorality, come from within, in the heart (Mark 7:14–23).

This reality is why it is so important that we think biblically about same-sex attraction in the way we are describing in this book. In order for real change to ensue, it is not enough for us to repent of homosexual behavior. We must repent of the desires that lead to behavior. The extent to which we disconnect homosexual desires from homosexual behavior is the same extent to which we will engage in mere behavior modification. To that extent, we would also fail to know the kind of real and lasting change promised in Scripture. If we want to help those who are

struggling with same-sex attraction, we must assert the sinfulness of homosexual behavior and desire. If we fail to do this, we
can expect more, not fewer, of the kinds of frustration that led
to the collapse of Exodus International.

A central reason why so many have tried and failed at their
efforts to change is that they have tried to do it without repentance. That is to say, they have pursued a path to change that
is different from the one that God lays out in his Word, that is
promised to be attended to with power by the Holy Spirit, and
that exalts Jesus Christ as the exclusive Savior from sin that he is.

Repentance Is the *Only* Path to Change

The only way any person can have change from any sin—
whether homosexuality or anything else—is by repentance. We
have talked about myths concerning change in this chapter.
In the next chapter we will talk about the very specific steps
that Christians must take as they walk the repentant path from
homosexuality to holiness.

Questions for Reflection

1. In what ways does ministry to people supplement a
   biblical understanding of ethics relating to same-sex
   attraction?
2. Think of your own life. What specific examples can you
   list in which you experienced the resurrecting power of
   the Holy Spirit to deliver you from personal sin?
3. In what ways is insisting on heterosexual conformity
   instead of conformity to holiness harmful to those who
   are struggling with same-sex attraction?
4. How do the different core priorities of reparative therapy
   fall short of producing biblical change within a person?

4

A Biblical Path to Change

Something tragic has happened in the way Christians think about the problems they face as they live their lives. Somewhere along the way, Christians started believing that the Bible is not about offering help with hugely complex and significant problems like same-sex attraction and behavior. Even though Christians cherish the Bible and embrace its authority, they unfortunately also seem to think it is rather beside the point when it comes to charting a course for change with hard problems like homosexuality.

If you are inclined to believe that we are overdoing it with that charge, then consider the books available on homosexuality that have been written from an evangelical perspective. As we have pointed out, many of them focus on the ethics of homosexuality with very little instruction about how to change homosexual desires. We are grateful for our Christian brothers and sisters who speak winsomely and faithfully about the biblical ethics of homosexual behavior. But we are also concerned that focusing on ethics to the exclusion of the ministry of change both reflects and provides an inaccurate picture that the Bible is all about ethical behavior and not much about how behavior can change.

Consider also the way Christians have relied on reparative therapy to help struggling people to change. As we argued in the last chapter, this therapy is unbiblical, obscures the glory of Christ, and is therefore ultimately unhelpful, even though its proponents have some success to report. The reason that so many Christians have looked to such an unbiblical approach for help makes a colossal statement about how Christians evaluate the resources available in Scripture. Christians look outside the text of Scripture for guidance in helping people to change because they find the resources within Scripture to be wanting. For at least these two reasons, therefore, it seems that Christians have undervalued Scripture's teaching about change with regard to same-sex attraction.

But, as we have said, the Bible is about more than ethics, and the resources in Scripture are not wanting when it comes to change. Furthermore, God did not provide us a Bible with only instruction about the small problems in the Christian life. Jesus means not only to redeem us from the "small" problems of grumbling, laziness, and prayerlessness. He also intends to redeem us from the massive and debilitating problems that push us to the brink of despair—problems like crippling anxiety, suicidal despair, and—yes—homosexuality.

When we come to the Bible, we need to read it not merely for help in these small problems, but for help in the large ones as well. We need to believe that what have been called the normal means of grace work for the massive problems of Christian living every bit as much as they work for the ones that do not make the headlines. The Bible's teaching on love, grace, repentance, forgiveness, the fellowship of believers, Scripture memory, how to worship, and a million other things are crucial for us as we change in every area of life with every problem that causes pain. We need to meditate on Scripture's practicality in this way. We must teach about it. We must implement it. As we do this, we will not need to look to methods of change that are outside the Bible and, therefore, devalue Christ. It is in this spirit that we write this chapter about how to use the normal means of grace in a typical chapter of the Bible to help same-sex–attracted men and women to know profound change.

In the last chapter, we discussed how repentance is central to change. Repentance is the Christ-centered path on which we take all the steps of change. In this chapter we want to examine Paul's teaching in Ephesians 5:1–21 to see what kinds of steps on the path of repentance lead to biblical change concerning same-sex attraction. Of course, it is impossible in one chapter to discuss all the things that are important in the change process for any serious sin struggle. Still, Ephesians 5 is rich with apostolic wisdom about change. There is more wisdom in one chapter of one book of the Bible about change than there is in all the volumes about reparative therapy put together. Paying careful attention to the kinds of practical work of repentance that Paul offers will allow for an extraordinary—and perhaps surprising—measure of progress.

Paths of Repentance in Ephesians 5

In Ephesians 5, Paul is explaining the ethical implications of the gospel of Jesus Christ, the same gospel he expounded in the earlier portion of the letter. The chapter is about how to live the new life that believers possess in Christ. Although the words "homosexual" or "same-sex attraction" do not appear in the text, this passage deals head-on with sexual immorality. Paul wrote this portion of his epistle intending us to apply its powerful principles to every problem we face, including the specific problem under consideration in this book. There is as much to learn in this passage about how to grow in grace concerning same-sex attraction as there is concerning any challenging problem. In this chapter, we will observe five steps that Paul urges us to take as we walk the repentant path toward change.

Repent of Hatred and Pursue Love

Paul begins his teaching in Ephesians 5 with a powerful exhortation. He says,

> Therefore be imitators of God, as beloved children. And walk in love as Christ loved us and gave himself up for us, a fragrant offering and sacrifice to God. (Eph. 5:1–2)

In these two verses of Scripture, the apostle describes both the goal and the ground of the repentant life. Paul indicates that the goal of the repentant life in Christ is one of walking in love. As Paul exhorts us to walk in love, he does not leave us curious about what this love should look like. We are pointed to Jesus Christ and his self-giving as the ultimate picture of Christian love. The goal of the Christian life is one of selfless and sacrificial love as exemplified in the life that Jesus Christ lived to serve sinners.

The call to walk in love has everything to do with biblical sexual ethics. God loves monogamous, life-long, heterosexual marriage because he loves us and wants us to experience the good and gracious fruit that comes from living in this righteous way. God's commands do not stem from any desire to be stingy concerning joy. Rather, they grow out of God's heart for us to know the fullness of happiness that he has for us in this life. That means that we engage in an act of love every time we desire to act out a sexuality that honors and upholds this biblical ethic. Every time we desire to act out a sexuality that undercuts such an ethic, we are engaging in an act of hate.

This is a point that is clearly in the front of Paul's mind, because immediately after he gives this command to love in Ephesians 5:1–2 he forbids sexual immorality, impurity, and covetousness in Ephesians 5:3. This means that, in Paul's thinking, one of the primary threats to this call to love is sexual immorality.

Homosexual desires and behaviors are clearly within these biblical categories of sexual immorality, defining them as unloving. When individuals with same-sex attraction desire to act in ways that violate this sexual ethic, they desire to act in ways that do spiritual harm to those who are the objects of their desire. It is often the case that those experiencing the desire to act in such a way do not think they are doing harm. Nevertheless, this harm is seen in the reality that same-sex desires and actions incur the wrath of God (1 Thess. 4:3–6). Desiring to act in such a way is to long for behaviors that would lead us and others to incur the wrath of God. Such a reality could never be understood as loving.

This biblical truth is why it is so misguided to claim that there are loving and positive benefits to patterns of homosexual desire, which are often called orientation. That is the neo-traditional error that has gained some influence in evangelical circles. When *WORLD* magazine published a profile of Julie Rodgers, a counselor at Wheaton College, Rodgers reflected this point of view. She acknowledged the sinfulness of homosexual behavior but not of homosexual orientation. *WORLD* reported her belief that

> same-sex orientation is not sinful. She said it can actually
> be "an expression of diversity, a unique way of experiencing
> art and beauty and community." Rodgers added that her "gay
> parts . . . overflow into compassion for marginalized people
> and empathy for social outcasts—[God has] used my gay way
> of being for His glory rather than making me straight."[1]

We contend that this neo-traditional perspective is out of step with biblical teaching. It is a matter of crucial importance that Christians should not rationalize sinful desire in this way. No Christian has ever been helped by seeking out the virtuous elements of his or her sinful tendencies. Such people are helped only as they confess their sin, ask God for his forgiveness, and trust in his grace to change. In this case that means surrendering any attempt to find the silver lining of same-sex attraction. It means confessing that this sin—like all others—is sinful. It means asking God for his gracious forgiveness in this regard. It means pleading with the Lord for the strength to love one's neighbor by fleeing sexual immorality rather than by rationalizing it. Repentance from same-sex attraction does not kill compassion toward the marginalized. Christ's love compels real compassion, but disordered sexual desire does not.

Rodgers has since left her post at Wheaton after announcing that she now views homosexual relationships as consistent with Christianity.[2] Her experience exposes the fundamental inconsistency at the heart of the neo-traditional approach. It affirms that same-sex orientation can be a moral good, even though same-sex behavior is a moral evil. At the heart of her neo-traditional view was an anthropological contradiction that does not survive biblical scrutiny. Our sexual attractions—even the ones that come naturally to us—are fundamentally moral in nature. And it makes no sense at all to say that same-sex behavior is sinful but that the attraction that leads to such behavior is not. Those who are trying to hold these irreconcilable propositions together are doing something risky. When someone like Rodgers accepts that "gay is good," we shouldn't be surprised when they eventually reach the conclusion that same-sex behavior is "good" as well. We celebrate neo-traditionalists who are living faithful lives of celibacy. Embracing celibacy is absolutely necessary for all unmarried Christians—same-sex–attracted or otherwise. But celibacy alone does not get at the heart of things. Biblical Christianity cannot be reduced to behavioral modification. Authentic Christianity results in people becoming obedient from the heart (Rom. 6:17). Embracing same-sex orientation as a moral good undermines such obedience and works against efforts to be celibate.

In Ephesians 5:1–2, Paul does not merely tell us to walk in love. In describing Christ as the goal for this life of love, Paul also describes him as the ground, or the foundation, of this life of love. Christ loved us and gave himself up for us, a fragrant offering and sacrifice to God.

This is the good news of the gospel. The call to walk in love is not an option. It is something we *must* do. But that is not good news. The reason it is not good news is that no person who struggles with same-sex attraction has the ability to walk in love on his own. The good news of Jesus Christ is that our Mediator laid down his life as a sacrifice to God for all who would trust in him. Jesus Christ fulfilled the demands of the law for all who trust in him in the loving sacrifice he made. All of us, regardless of sexual orientation, have in Christ a Savior who secures our pardon from sin and our ability to grow in grace and, ultimately, to reflect his own righteousness.

The effort to defend the sinlessness of homosexual orientation today is well intended. The motivation seems to be to provide compassion to same-sex–attracted men and women. The compassionate motive is to create a space in their desires that is not dirty, sinful, and guilty. The impulse here is to offer good news that you're not as bad as you have been told you are. We understand this impulse and appreciate the compassion behind it. In one sense, it is true. Singling out same-sex–attracted people as especially sinful undersells the deep sinfulness that marks all of us. But in another sense, it is not true. It does not help anyone to give sinners the impression that their sin is not sin. This is not the kind of good news that the Bible ever offers to anyone with any sin struggle. In fact, it is at odds with the Christian gospel. Christians have never tried to help sinners by providing the false assurance that sin is not as bad as they have believed. They have, instead, pointed to a Savior who offers forgiveness more amazing than we can fathom. The truth is that persons with same-sex attraction, like all of us, are far more sinful than they have been told. Humbly confessing this reality is the only way to experience the full, saving love of Jesus Christ. This is the good news of the love of Jesus Christ that sets sinners free and gives them his own resources to love the way he does.

The good news for all of us sinners is that there is enough grace to cover all our sins. When we feel overwhelmed by a sin that we don't know how to stop—there's grace from Jesus for that. When we are driven to despair by a sinful disposition that we feel we have never chosen—there's grace from Jesus for that. When we sense that turning from a dominating sin might lead us to a place where we don't even know who we are—there's grace from Jesus for that, too. The good news of the love of Jesus Christ means that grace is always greater than all of our sin. Jesus lived. Jesus died. Jesus rose. Those realities are the foundation of the truth that "Where sin increases, grace abounds all the more" (see Rom. 5:20).

It is this reality of the love of Jesus Christ for sinners that will empower the repentance from hatred to love. It is the same reality that will empower every other step on the path to repentance that we will consider.

Repent of Covetousness and Pursue Gratitude

Paul progresses in Ephesians from love to gratitude. In Ephesians 5:3–4 he says,

> But sexual immorality and all impurity or covetousness must not even be named among you, as is proper among saints.

Let there be no filthiness nor foolish talk nor crude joking,
which are out of place, but instead let there be thanksgiving.

In this passage, Paul forbids all manner of sinful sexual expressions including impurity, filthiness, crude joking, and others. The two most relevant for us are sexual immorality and covetousness.

One of the main goals in this book has been to show that same-sex sexual attraction, not just homosexual behavior, is sinful. One of the evidences of that—beyond what we have already seen—is found right here in this passage. Paul teaches that at the root of sexual immorality is covetousness. The Greek word translated here is different from the one for *desire* that we examined earlier. The word used here has a different nuance and means to desire more than is one's due.[3] To be covetous is to desire more than God has given you. In areas of sexuality, if you desire more than you have been given, then you will, sooner or later, engage in acts of sexual immorality. A person who identifies with a homosexual orientation is a person who desires more, either relationally or physically, from the same sex than what God says is good for such a person to have.

Paul, however, does not merely tell us something that we need to stop doing. He also tells us how to replace it. In place of sexual immorality, impurity, and covetousness, Paul tells us to put on thanksgiving. Instead of coveting, we are to be filled with gratitude. The divine logic here is magnificent when you stop to think about it. The spiritual opposite of a covetous desire for more is a grateful heart for all that God has given, and no more. The covetous heart looks at what it has received and lusts for more. The grateful heart looks at what God has provided, is overwhelmed with contentment, and says, "Thank you."

As same-sex–attracted men and women walk the path of repentance toward change, one of the most practical things they can do is to be thankful. Perhaps you are in the throes of a significant struggle and wonder what there is to be grateful for. Here is a thought to get you started.

Be thankful for God's unflinching purpose to make you like Christ. When your flesh screams out to be indulged, when you feel isolated and alone, when you wish you had any problem other than the one you have got, remember that a good and sovereign God sent this problem into your life to make you more like Christ. God will never waste your struggle. He is sanctifying you. Be grateful, therefore, as you remember the words of 1 Peter 1:3–7.

> Blessed be the God and Father of our Lord Jesus Christ! According to his great mercy, he has caused us to be born again to a living hope through the resurrection of Jesus Christ from the dead, to an inheritance that is imperishable, undefiled, and unfading, kept in heaven for you, who by God's power are being guarded through faith for a salvation ready to be revealed in the last time. In this you rejoice, though now for a little while, if necessary, you have been grieved by various trials, so that the tested genuineness of your faith—more precious than gold that perishes though it is tested by fire—may be found to result in praise and glory and honor at the revelation of Jesus Christ.

Consider all that there is to fuel gratitude in this passage! God has an inheritance in heaven for you. He is guarding you for that inheritance, but, as you wait, the genuineness of your faith is tested by fiery trials. Fire is painful, and trials hurt—but they are necessary.

This passage raises a very hard and important question that you must answer: how would you ever know whether you love God or instead love what God gives you? This question is a hard question to answer. Every good thing that you enjoy comes from God, and so how are you to separate the gift from the giver? How do you know if you have genuine love for God or if you love only the good things God gives you? This question is also important to answer, because if you love God's gifts more than you love God, you are an idolater, and the inheritance waiting in heaven for believers is not for you. So, to put the question another way: how do you know whether you are an idolater or a Christian?

Peter tells us the answer to this question in the first chapter of his epistle. You know that you love God and not God's gifts when he takes the good gifts away and your faith remains. This is how fiery trials test the genuineness of your faith. God is actually kind when he demonstrates the genuineness of your faith by stripping everything else away. When all but God is lost and you still love God, it demonstrates the certainty of your faith.

This is often a hard teaching, because we love comfort more than pain. When we are tempted to think this way, we need to remember from 1 Peter that comfort is the very thing that threatens genuine faith. How unkind God would be to let us rest easy and comfortable and die with an idolatrous faith in created things rather than in the Creator.

It is also a hard teaching because we sometimes think that we would rather have the trials of another than the ones we actually have. But this is the exact same thing as the previous concern, just stated in different language. The point is that we want something less painful. We want something that we judge to be easier to bear. In those moments we must remember that it is in our weakness that God's strength is shown (2 Cor. 12:9).

In every trial, God is loving us by leading us closer to himself. Every Christian must always be thankful for every trial sooner or later. You must be thankful for the experience of God's grace, which is possible in the midst of the sting of your same-sex attraction. If you trust him and draw near to him, Jesus will give you the grace to be thankful for God's work in proving the genuineness of your faith. When your flesh burns from unfulfilled same-sex desire, quench the flames with the balm of gratitude for God's gracious trial, which proves that you are in Christ.

Repent of Sinful Presumption and Pursue Discipleship

After Paul encourages Christians to replace sexual immorality with gratitude, he gives one of the most sobering warnings in the New Testament.

> For you may be sure of this, that everyone who is sexually immoral or impure, or who is covetous [that is, an idolater] has no inheritance in the kingdom of Christ and God. Let no one deceive you with empty words, for because of these things the wrath of God comes upon the sons of disobedience. Therefore do not become partners with them; for at one time you were darkness, but now you are light in the Lord. Walk as children of light. (Eph. 5:5–8)

In Ephesians 5:3–4, Paul said that sexual immorality, impurity, and covetousness must not even be named among Christians. Now he raises the stakes with a warning. Paul makes change in behavior and change in desires a crucial test of our salvation. His point is that our walking in the light is crucial evidence of whether we are actually living in the light. You can't know Jesus and make a habit of sinning. People who would say you can do this are guilty of spreading the empty words that Paul cautions against. Real faith in Jesus produces the fruit of Jesus in your walk.

We live in a Christian culture that is often very nervous about talking about behavior. There is a concern that if we talk about what we do, we will detract from what Christ has done for us.

We understand that. One of the central realities of Christianity is that Christ has done for us what we could not do for ourselves, namely, fulfill the law's demands. We do not ever want to detract from the glory of Christ by focusing on our effort to the exclusion of his work for us. Nevertheless, one of the things that Christ has done for us is to secure our obedience. Christ does more than forgive us our sins. He changes our life so that we can walk the way he walked (1 John 2:6).

This means it is presumptuous to persist in sin while professing that we are in Christ. The authors of the New Testament wrote warning passages like this one precisely so we would not do that. If you are a professing Christian and you are persisting in unrepentant same-sex desires or behavior, you need to be alarmed by this passage. The change in your walk is evidence of the change in your heart toward Christ. If there is never any change in your walk, then you have no reason to believe that there has ever been a change in your heart toward God.

It is important to think through what this walk—this change in behavior—would look like for a Christian who is struggling with same-sex attraction. Of course, you should stay away from tempting people and places. You might have to change how you spend your time and whom you spend your time with. Change will be required in what you watch on television. You will have to limit some of your freedoms, such as your access to the Internet. You will do all these things and more.[4] There is something more profound, however, that needs to change about your walk.

The Bible uses a number of different metaphors to talk about a life of discipleship in which we follow in Jesus' steps. One of those metaphors is the one of walking, which Paul uses here. Another metaphor that the apostle John uses is one of abiding. In John 15:1-10, John reports the teaching of Jesus in which we are instructed to abide in Christ, just as a branch abides in a vine. Jesus teaches that the way we abide in him is by reading the Bible and praying (John 15:7).[5]

If Bible reading and prayer sound too simplistic to be a crucial tool in the desperate fight against same-sex attraction, then consider a few realities. Consider that the Word of God is powerful, sharper than any double-edged sword. Consider that this powerful Word of God is the exclusive deposit of truth that, when hidden in your heart, will keep you from sinning against God (Ps. 119:11). Consider also that God has given the gift of prayer so that you can draw near to him in any time of temptation and despair. When sin clings so closely that you believe there is no way to be free, remember that God is yet closer and that you can call to him in prayer.

Bible reading and prayer are the necessary means that God has given us to draw near to him. They are also crucial weapons as we seek to take our sinful thoughts captive to obey Christ in the midst of temptation (2 Cor. 10:5). And, more than that, they can provide assurance of faith even when progress against our sexual sin seems slow. Here is one example of how this is true.

You may have felt despair as you read about the warning in Ephesians that your faith must be reflected in your obedient walking with Christ. Perhaps you sense that you have faith in Jesus, but you see a lot of struggle against sexual sin in your life, and it makes you despair that you are unsaved. We know what that feels like. Every Christian has been there at one point or another. In those moments, the Bible and prayer are your friends. In 1 John 1:5–10, John is telling Christians how to walk in the light. He says that you cannot walk in the light while denying your sin. The only way to walk in the light is to confess the sin that you commit and to trust that Christ has paid for it. We often think that we are walking in the light when our lives are sin free. John says that this is not the case. The people who walk in the light are not the people who are not guilty of sin. The people who walk in the light are the people who pray, confessing the sin that they actually commit.

Are you struggling with same-sex attraction and behavior? Does progress seem slow? Does salvation seem far off? Do you feel clueless about how someone like you could ever be saved? First John gives you hope that you do not have to be perfect to have a walk with Christ that reflects faith. You just have to have a heart that runs to your Father, pleading for forgiveness. When you do this in faith, you will have the forgiveness that he promises, and you will be walking the path that Jesus desires for you to walk. Ironically, it is the people who presumptuously think they're doing fine who are in the most trouble in the kingdom of God (1 Cor. 10:12). Fight against this, repenting of such presumption and walking with Christ in Bible reading and repentant prayer.

Repent of Sinful Concealing and Pursue Open Accountability

Every struggling person we have ever known who returned to a homosexual lifestyle is someone who came to be dishonest and deceptive about some element of the sin struggle being experienced. This is why Paul expands on his previous teaching in the following way:

Take no part in the unfruitful works of darkness, but instead expose them. For it is shameful even to speak of the things that they do in secret. But when anything is exposed by the light, it becomes visible, for anything that becomes visible is light. (Eph. 5:11–14)

Paul stresses that the way to walk in the light is to expose the darkness to light. There is no way for you to walk righteously while concealing the darkness from the shining light of Christ. If you are like most people, you know that this is true but find it hard to actually do it. You believe you can't share the secret struggle that you face. You are tired of burdening your friends with your secret thoughts. You lie to yourself that the current inner struggle isn't a very big deal and will eventually go away.

All these excuses are deceptions that keep you from doing what God commands in Ephesians. They will eventually lead to your downfall. To combat this, one of the most important things you can do is to find a fellow Christian of the same sex with whom you can be close and completely honest and who will feel absolutely no temptation to engage in a sexual relationship with you. When you find this person, you need to resolve to follow his or her counsel and to tell him or her *everything*. You need to say when you're tempted, how regularly you're tempted, what your past struggles have been, who tempts you, and any other relevant details.

If you're like most people, however, you need less instruction about what to do and more encouragement about why you should do it. You likely know that you need a relationship like this, and yet you struggle to begin one. Let us give you three motivations to pursue this kind of relationship.

First, as we have already seen, the only way to walk in the light is by confessing sin. The reason we don't confess our sin to God and others is because we are ashamed that our sin somehow makes us different from everyone else. You don't want to share your shameful secrets with someone who you think doesn't have shameful secrets. The truth of sin is that we all have shameful secrets. The exhortation to us as Christians is that we all need to be confessing our darkness to someone who can help. You will never confess your hidden sins to someone who does not have a very long list of his own. We really are in this together, and we need each other.

Second, Jesus is the one whose opinion about you ultimately matters. He sees all your sins, loves you, and died for those sins. In your sin, Jesus loved you and died for you. There is nothing left for you to cover up. If you are a believer, Jesus has already covered your sin in his blood. That means that when you confess your sins, you are confessing things that the most important person in the universe already knows about and already paid for. What can man do to you when God is for you (Rom. 8:33–34)?

Finally, if you don't walk in the light, the warnings of this passage will apply to you. If you do not walk as Jesus walked, you will prove that you never knew Jesus. Which is worse? To experience the fleeting shame of exposing your hidden sins to someone who loves you and wants to help? Or to experience separation from Christ forever as you pay the penalty for those hidden sins?

Jesus loves you and wants to help you. That is why this command is in the Bible. You need to repent of your sinful concealing of sin, trust Christ, and ask for his grace to tell the truth to a wise Christian brother or sister.

Repent of Cold Hearts and Pursue Singing to Jesus

Any area where we struggle with sin and unrighteousness is an area of coldness in our soul. That means that, where you find struggles with sin, you need to fight to ignite your heart with the grace of Jesus Christ. There are all kinds of ways to do this. In fact, we have already discussed some ways, including pursuing gratitude, Bible reading and prayer, and even accountability. Paul gives another strategy in this text, however, as he exhorts us to "be filled with the Spirit, addressing one another in psalms and hymns and spiritual songs, singing and making melody to the Lord with your heart" (Eph. 5:18–19).

As Paul shows us how to walk in the grace we have received in Jesus Christ, he commands us to sing. Have you ever considered that God has, in a fascinating way, wired our affections to music? This is why 150 chapters of the Bible are inspired music in the book of Psalms. Singing the truths of Scripture has an ability to warm our soul like few other things can. In her stimulating memoir of conversion to Christ, Rosaria Butterfield expresses how important singing the Psalms has been to her own sanctification and growth. She says that her church's singing of the Psalms transformed her perspective.

> I became convinced that the worship of the Lord was the most important thing that we can do. Notice: I did not say that it is the only thing that we can do. But worship is the launching pad for life. And, through it, God equips us to do Kingdom work in the world. Therefore, worship has to be right in God's eyes and right in our hearts and minds. . . . I fell in love and gratitude with our denomination's worship standards, seeing it as foundational, not to our salvation, but to our sanctification and our service.[6]

Singing songs of praise to God is one real "secret" of growing in holiness. The next time you are tempted, or are feeling lonely, or sense that you are overwhelmed with despair, try singing,

> Jesus! what a friend for sinners!
> Jesus, Lover of my soul;
> Friends may fail me, foes assail me,
> He my Savior makes me whole.
> Hallelujah! what a Savior!
> Hallelujah! what a friend!
> Saving, helping, keeping, loving,
> He is with me to the end.

If you prefer something more contemporary, you can try singing "The Power of the Cross" by Keith Getty and Stuart Townend. It doesn't matter what year the song was written, as long as it directs your heart to true things about Jesus Christ. When you are in a tempting situation, don't let your heart be drawn into the temptation, but pray and fight for grace to sing. Sing songs that remind you of who Jesus is and what he did for you. Sing songs that remind you of who you are in him. We live in a wonderful day full of reminders from believers that we ought to be preaching the gospel to ourselves. That is a glorious exhortation. Paul adds to that here by saying we ought to sing the gospel to ourselves. Trust us on this one. Singing the truths of Scripture to yourself has dramatic power to fix the gospel in your heart. God can use it powerfully to change you.

The Gospel Really Changes You

If you have been a Christian for any length of time, you may have read this chapter without finding anything dramatically new. The things we have talked about in this chapter are all quite normal. Perhaps you're looking for the new approach, the silver bullet that will take away all your striving. You need to know that, as God changes you, he will not do it with something really new. God will change you by something really old. There is no power to change in extra-biblical approaches like reparative therapy. There is power in the gospel as we lay hold of it by growing in love, gratitude, discipleship, and accountability, and as our hearts grow warm from singing praise to God. Do not let these strategies seem lifeless! These are the strategies that the living God has inspired to bring change in your life! There are other strategies in other places in God's Word, but there are five in this chapter. These are God's normal means for you to grow in his grace. He gave them to you so you could change as you grow in knowing him. As you fight to employ these strategies, you can know that, whether your path to change leads to marriage or singleness, whether it is easy or difficult, Christ will be with you, giving you more joy as you kill sin than you could ever have by indulging it.

Questions for Reflection

1. What factors contribute to people's belief that they must go outside the Bible to find the necessary resources to address the "large" problems of life, such as same-sex attraction?

2. How is it more compassionate to affirm the sinfulness of one's same-sex attraction than to deny it?

3. How does the command to "count it all joy, my brothers, when you meet trials of various kinds" (James 1:2) help to spur on repentance from covetousness and pursuit of gratitude?

4. Why is accountability and confession of personal sin essential to living in repentance of same-sex attraction?

5. How can you seek to employ the strategies discussed in this chapter within your own life to fight and resist sin in order to pursue holiness?

5

How Evangelicals Can Change

So far in this book, we have been discussing how someone battling homosexual attractions should think about biblical change. We have made the case that transformation into the image of Christ needs to happen from the inside out. Biblical change includes not only a transformation of sinful deeds but also a reordering of fallen desires. The gospel provides everything that same-sex–attracted people need to make this kind of change a reality in their lives.

But same-sex–attracted people are not the only ones who need to change. Evangelical Christians have certainly had a spotted record when it comes to addressing the issue of homosexuality. Our churches have not always been the welcoming places that they should have been for sinners—especially for those struggling with same-sex attraction. Many same-sex–attracted youth growing up in evangelical churches have felt isolated, alone, and bewildered by their attractions and have found little help from their own churches. Instead they have encountered much in the way of politics and stigma but very little in the way of help and hope. This kind of ministry is unfaithful, and we need to do better. In short, we need to change too.

So evangelicals would do well to rethink how we speak not only about LGBT issues but also—and more importantly—about people struggling with these issues.[1] Sometimes our ministry is hindered when we misunderstand the possibilities for faithfulness. And unfortunately people committed to normalizing homosexual behavior force a false dichotomy regarding this issue: the intolerance option and the tolerance option.

The *intolerance option* is the idea that, if you oppose homosexuality in any way, then you are intolerant of gay people as persons. You hate both homosexuality *and* homosexuals. You don't think that they deserve basic respect as persons, and you think that they don't even deserve civil rights. If your religion tells you that homosexuality is wrong, then you and your religion are bigoted because you promote hate against homosexuals. This is the intolerance option.

The *tolerance option* is the idea that the only way to show love and compassion to gay people is to recognize that homosexuality is morally acceptable. You must affirm not only that homosexual persons have civil rights but also that the lifestyle itself is a wonderful option for those who are so inclined. You have to affirm the persons *and* the lifestyle if you want to be truly tolerant.

The tolerance option and the intolerance option are regularly set before us as the only possible choices we have in relating to our same-sex–attracted friends and neighbors. Since none of us wants to be bigoted or hateful, we feel a tremendous pressure from our culture to choose the tolerance option. After all, who wants to be a bigot?

But our question is this. Are these really the only two options? Is it true that our only options are either to hate our same-sex–attracted neighbors or to affirm them? This is a false choice. There is another option. It is the *biblical option*, and it also happens to be the one that is the most loving. Biblically defined, love will determine both *what* we speak and *how* we speak when we minister to people who experience same-sex attraction. In saying this, our concern in this chapter is not with how to fight the larger culture war that is going on over homosexuality in general or gay marriage in particular. Christians have a role to play in that discussion, but that is not our aim in this chapter. Our aim is for us to consider how we, as Christians, are to address the gospel to those who struggle with same-sex sexual desires.

Ephesians 4:14–15 says that

> we are no longer to be children, tossed here and there by
> waves, and carried about by every wind of doctrine, by the
> trickery of men, by craftiness in deceitful scheming; but
> speaking the truth in love, we are to grow up in all aspects
> into Him, who is the head, even Christ. (NASB)

So we are called to *speak the truth in love*. There is much that
we could say about what it looks like to speak the truth in love.
But we want to focus on three specific exhortations that grow out
of the three New Testament texts that explicitly address homosexuality: (1) speak the truth, (2) speak the gospel, and (3) speak
humility. These are obligations that each of us have if we want
to be faithful ambassadors of Christ in our ministry, whether to
same-sex–attracted neighbors or to same-sex–attracted brothers
and sisters in our churches.

Speak the Truth (Romans 1:26–27)

Speaking the truth means simply speaking what the Bible says
about homosexuality. One of the first things you will encounter
when you try to speak the truth is that people generally resist
it. This should not be surprising. People are sinners. Sinners
sin. And that includes the sin of opposing the truth. In fact, the
apostle Paul says in Romans 1:18 that sinners as a rule "suppress
the truth in unrighteousness" (NASB). The truth convicts us of
sin, and, apart from God's grace, we all resist that conviction.
Jesus says it this way:

> This is the judgment, that the Light has come into the world,
> and men loved the darkness rather than the Light, for their
> deeds were evil. For everyone who does evil hates the Light,

and does not come to the Light, for fear that his deeds will be exposed. (John 3:19-20 NASB)

Sinners don't like the light, so when they are confronted with the truth they suppress it. Sinners suppress biblical truth by saying one of two things: (1) that the Bible doesn't mean what you think it means, or (2) that the Bible is not trustworthy. The liberal and revisionist approaches that we mentioned at the beginning of this book suppress the truth in precisely these two ways. If we would be faithful followers of Christ, we must not fall into either one of those errors. Instead, there are at least two truths that we should be clear about with respect to homosexuality from Romans 1:26-27: (1) that it is sin, and (2) that it is a judgment.

Homosexuality as Sin (1:26b-27)

For their women exchanged the natural function for that which is unnatural, and in the same way also the men abandoned the natural function of the woman and burned in their desire toward one another, men with men committing indecent acts and receiving in their own persons the due penalty of their error. (Rom. 1:26b-27 NASB)

According to this text, both women and men who abandon the "natural function" of sexuality to engage in same-sex acts are committing sin. There are some who will tell you that "natural" refers to one's sexual orientation, that this verse condemns only people who participate in same-sex activity and who have a heterosexual orientation, and that it is not a sin for those who do so "naturally"— those who act in accordance with their own homosexual orientation.

But that's not what Paul is talking about, is it? For Paul, "natural" is defined not by one's personal orientation (whatever that may be) but by God's intention in creation. For Paul, what is "natural" is defined by what we see in the garden of Eden before the fall: one man and one woman in the covenant of marriage. Any other kind of union is "unnatural" and sinful in Paul's way of thinking. Paul couldn't be any clearer here. Homosexuality goes against God's design and is a sin.

Homosexuality as Judgment (1:26a)

> For this reason God gave them over to degrading passions. (Rom. 1:26a NASB)

The sin of idolatry—creature worship—is mentioned in verse 25. Paul says that, because humans were idolaters, God judged them by giving them over to "degrading passions." We do not desire the sexual ideal given in the garden of Eden. All of us are inclined (to one extent or another) toward perversions. We have degrading passions. In verse 26, the specific "degrading passion" is homosexual desire.

When we deal with sinners in general and gay sinners in particular, we do them no favors by running away from the truth of Scripture. We have to tell them clearly—even when it is unpopular—that homosexual acts are sinful and that homosexual passions are a judgment.

If we withhold that truth from them out of fear of offending them, then we don't love them. We cut them off from salvation. The only way for them to be saved is to receive Christ. The only way to receive Christ is by *repentance* and *faith*. They cannot repent if we enable them to suppress the truth in unrighteousness. We must shine the light. They will either come to it or flee from it. We cannot control their response. We must speak the truth if we love them.

Speak the Gospel (1 Corinthians 6:9–11)

Christ intends to save same-sex–attracted people from their sin and to include them in his body, the church. No text brings this truth out more vividly than 1 Corinthians 6:9–11. We want you to see three things in this text.

The Unrighteous Are Excluded from God's Kingdom (6:9a)

> Or do you not know that the unrighteous will not inherit the kingdom of God? (1 Cor. 6:9a NASB)

The kingdom of God is not for everyone. Not everyone gets in. Those who die in their sin will perish for eternity. They do not experience God's redemptive reign through Christ. Because they are unrighteous, they are *excluded*.

Homosexual Sinners Are Among the Unrighteous Who Are Excluded (6:9b–10)

> Do not be deceived; neither fornicators, nor idolaters, nor adulterers, nor effeminate, nor homosexuals, nor thieves, nor the covetous, nor drunkards, nor revilers, nor swindlers, will inherit the kingdom of God. (1 Cor. 6:9b–10 NASB)

Homosexual sinners are named among those who are unrighteous and excluded. The terms translated "effeminate" and "homosexual" in the NASB refer to the passive and active partners in a homosexual encounter. And these two are included in a long list of other kinds of sinners: fornicators, idolaters, adulterers, thieves, the covetous people, drunkards, revilers, and swindlers. It is a bad crew, and homosexual sinners are named right there with them.

The Gospel Makes Them Righteous and Included (6:11)

> Such were some of you; but you were washed, but you were sanctified, but you were justified in the name of the Lord Jesus Christ and in the Spirit of our God. (1 Cor. 6:11 NASB)

God is in the business of saving sinners—same-sex–attracted people included. We have disagreed with Wesley Hill on some issues in this book, but we are so grateful for the testimony he shares in his 2010 book *Washed and Waiting: Reflections on Christian Faithfulness and Homosexuality*. In the book, Hill describes his own lifelong struggle with homosexuality. For as long as he can remember, he has experienced a powerful and abiding attraction to persons of the same sex. There was no experience that triggered it. It has just been there from his earliest memories.

Hill also describes himself as a Christian. He became a follower of Jesus as a child, and he has never turned back from that commitment. He also agrees with what the Bible teaches about homosexuality—that it is a sin. So, against the powerful attractions that he feels every day, he agrees with the Bible against his feelings that sex is to be enjoyed only within the covenant of marriage. And so his life is one of radical self-denial. He is remaining celibate in faithfulness to Christ.

Why is he pursuing this path? He explains:

> In the end, what keeps me on the path I've chosen is not so much individual proof texts from Scripture or the sheer weight of the church's traditional teaching against homosexual practice. Instead, it is, I think, those texts and traditions and teachings as I see them from within the true story of what God has done in Jesus Christ— and the whole perspective on life and the world that flows from that story, as expressed definitively in Scripture. Like a piece from a jigsaw puzzle finally locked into its rightful place, the Bible and the church's no to homosexual behavior make sense to me—it has the ring of truth . . . when I look at it as one piece within the larger Christian narrative. I abstain from homosexual behavior because of the power of that scriptural story.[2]

For him, 1 Corinthians 6:9 is a part of that story. He is *washed* and he is *waiting* for the day when disordered desires will be taken away.

Do not be surprised when someone comes to you at your church and says that she was saved out of a homosexual lifestyle. Do not be surprised when a young person who has grown up in the church says that he has been wrestling with these kinds of attractions. Jesus loves these dear people and saves them. Love them, pray for them, be compassionate toward them, and do everything you can to help them in their fight against this sin. But don't be surprised or stand aloof.

For those who you know outside the church who are same-sex attracted, make it your aim to win them to Christ. Love them like you would any other sinner. Speak the gospel to them so that they might be saved. And never do anything that would hinder the progress of the gospel in their lives. No bullying. No making fun. No gay jokes or name-calling. Only love, compassion, prayer, friendship, and good will.

The gospel of the Lord Jesus Christ provides for every sinner to be righteous and included in Christ's church. We should relate to our same-sex–attracted friends and neighbors as if we believe that.

Speak Humility (1 Timothy 1:8–17)

By this we mean speak with humility. Notice that Paul labels "homosexuals" as sinners in 1 Timothy 1:10.

> Realizing the fact that law is not made for a righteous person, but for those who are lawless and rebellious, for the ungodly and sinners, for the unholy and profane, for those who kill their fathers or mothers, for murderers and immoral men and homosexuals and kidnappers and liars and perjurers, and whatever else is contrary to sound teaching, according to the glorious gospel of the blessed God, with which I have been entrusted. (1 Tim. 1:9–11 NASB)

He includes homosexuals in a long list of sinners who are *lawless, rebellious, ungodly, unholy, and profane.* They are listed among a bad lot: those who kill their fathers or mothers, murderers, kidnappers, liars, and perjurers. Can there be any question about Paul's view of the moral status of homosexuality? Nevertheless, Paul still thinks himself to be the worst sinner of the lot (1:15–16).

It is a trustworthy statement, deserving full acceptance, that Christ Jesus came into the world to save sinners, among whom I am foremost of all. Yet for this reason I found mercy, so that in me as the foremost, Jesus Christ might demonstrate His perfect patience as an example for those who would believe in Him for eternal life. (1 Tim. 1:15–16 NASB)

When we say, "Speak humility," we mean that you need to speak the way that Paul speaks. Paul calls homosexuality sin. But when he does, he still thinks of himself as the biggest sinner on the planet. In this sense, it does not really matter who the biggest sinner is in reality. In your own heart, you ought always to feel like you are the biggest one, the worst of the lot. You ought to feel continually humbled by the fact that God deigned to have mercy on you. We do not speak to same-sex–attracted people as if we are without sin. We speak as sinners. So we speak with compassion and humility.

Final Exhortations to Love

We are often presented with a false choice concerning the church's ministry to same-sex–attracted people. We are told that we can either walk the path of homophobia and hatred, or can surrender our ancient beliefs to affirm homosexual practice. But this is an unnecessary dilemma. There is another way. We can love and minister to same-sex–attracted people while still holding fast to biblical truth. The world is going to stand against you as you try to love your neighbor in this way. Most people are not going to let you "love the sinner and hate the sin." And yet there is no other way to love and to be faithful to Jesus in this fallen world. The only people we have to love are sinners. That is what we all are. And yet we must learn to love people while not loving the ways in which they are unfaithful to God. That is how we must love, because that is how God has loved us (Rom. 5:8).

To that end, we close with ten exhortations on how we might love our same-sex–attracted neighbors better than we have.

1. Be a friend.

And by that, we mean be a real friend. Don't make changing your same-sex–attracted neighbor a condition of your friendship.

> A friend loves at all times,
> And a brother is born for adversity. (Prov. 17:17 NASB)

2. Listen.

Your same-sex–attracted neighbor may have a story to tell, and you need to hear it. Not just for his sake, but for yours. There is nothing better to wipe away erroneous caricatures than to listen to someone else's story. Listening does not equal approving an unbiblical ideology. It just means that you care and are open to learning.

> He who gives an answer before he hears,
> It is folly and shame to him. (Prov. 18:13 NASB)

3. Feel compassion.

Understand that your same-sex–attracted neighbors often feel distress over unwanted same-sex attraction. They can feel a real sense of alienation from their own sexual desires. For some, the experience is quite agonizing. How would you feel if you had to walk a mile in their shoes? We all experience some measure of brokenness due to the fallenness of creation. So we too know what it means to groan (Rom. 8:23). If this is true, it ought to summon forth a compassionate response to our same-sex–attracted neighbors.

> So, as those who have been chosen of God, holy and beloved, put on a heart of compassion, kindness, humility, gentleness and patience. (Col. 3:12 NASB)

4. Share the gospel.

The gospel is good news for sinners. It is the true story about a Creator God who loves sinners and who has made a way to reconcile them to himself through the death and resurrection of his own Son. It's the best news in the world. How could we possibly withhold that from any friend?

> Now all these things are from God, who reconciled us to Himself through Christ and gave us the ministry of reconciliation, namely, that God was in Christ reconciling the world to Himself, not counting their trespasses against them, and He has committed to us the word of reconciliation. (2 Cor. 5:18–19 NASB)

5. Speak the truth.

We are called not to participate in the unfruitful deeds of darkness, but instead to "expose them" (Eph. 5:11). That means we must always "speak the truth in love" (Eph. 5:18). We must realize that real love never evades the truth but always "rejoices with the truth" (1 Cor. 13:6). So loving our neighbors means telling them the truth, even when that truth brings an unpleasant confrontation.

You don't have to be mean, angry, or haughty to speak truthfully. You can do it in a way that is winsome and that shows concern but does not disdain. In short, you can speak the truth in love.

> But speaking the truth in love, we are to grow up in all aspects into Him who is the head, even Christ. (Eph. 4:15 NASB)

6. Be candid about differences.

This is a necessary corollary to speaking the truth. A true friend will always find a way to communicate differences that matter. A friendship that glosses over such things can degenerate into flattery and superficiality. Sometimes the truth about God's Word brings a confrontation, no matter how nice and compassionate you try to be in delivering it. But don't let the fear of confrontation keep you from being candid.

> Faithful are the wounds of a friend,
> But deceitful are the kisses of an enemy. (Prov. 27:6 NASB)

That means that an enemy will tell you what you want to hear, but a real friend will tell you what you need to hear. Sometimes saying the right thing is hard, but we won't shrink back from the confrontation if we really love our neighbor.

7. Oppose bullying.

Christians must lead the charge to condemn acts of abuse or bullying committed against our same-sex–attracted neighbors. Take your stand with the oppressed. Speak up for them. Do it even if it costs you social capital or risks subjecting yourself to the same bullying. This is the kind of sacrificial love that bears witness to the way Christ has loved us.

My son, if sinners entice you,

Do not consent.

If they say, "Come with us,

Let us lie in wait for blood,

Let us ambush the innocent without cause."

. . . .

My son, do not walk in the way with them.

Keep your feet from their path,

For their feet run to evil

And they hasten to shed blood. (Prov. 1:10–11; 15–16 NASB)

8. Receive your brothers and sisters.

We should befriend our same-sex–attracted neighbors even if they are not Christians. Some of them will repent of their sin, trust Christ, and become Christians. When they do, be prepared to rejoice and to receive them with open arms as brothers and sisters in Christ. Make sure they know that they are received as full members into the body of Christ even if they have ongoing struggles with same-sex attraction.

For by one Spirit we were all baptized into one body, whether Jews or Greeks, whether slaves or free, and we were all made to drink of one Spirit. (1 Cor. 12:13 NASB)

9. Strengthen your brothers and sisters.

Some new converts may experience a complete deliverance from same-sex attraction. Others may continue to struggle. Be prepared to walk with the strugglers and to strengthen them for what may be a very difficult obedience. God has given them everything that they need for life and godliness (2 Peter 1:3), and a part of God's provision for them is your friendship and encouragement.

But encourage one another day after day, as long as it is still called "Today," so that none of you will be hardened by the deceitfulness of sin. (Heb. 3:13 NASB)

10. Pray.

The Devil wants to destroy. Jesus wants to save (John 10:10). Pray for your same-sex–attracted neighbor that Jesus might have his way. In his own prayer for wayward Peter, Jesus modeled how we might intercede:

Behold, Satan has demanded permission to sift you like wheat; but I have prayed for you, that your faith may not fail. (Luke 22:31–32 NASB)

In a book called *Transforming Homosexuality*, in which we are discussing the importance of change in the life of those who are same-sex attracted, it is appropriate that we close by emphasizing the need we all have to grow in grace. It is clear that we all stand together in need of the mercy of God to forgive and to transform. Indeed, God's aim is to transform all his children into the image of his Son Jesus, who loved us and gave himself for us (2 Cor. 3:18). This book is offered with a prayer, therefore, that God would complete that work in all of us.

Questions for Reflection

1. Is it loving to withhold the truth of God's Word about sin and judgment? Why?
2. How does Paul model in 1 Timothy 1:15–16 the humility that we should have regarding our own sin?
3. Of the ten concluding practical exhortations, which ones do you need to work on cultivating most in your life toward others?

Notes

Preface: Why Do We Need This Book?

1. For a comprehensive account of the Bible's teaching about homosexuality, see Robert A. J. Gagnon, *The Bible and Homosexual Practice: Texts and Hermeneutics* (Nashville: Abingdon, 2001). At the popular level, we recommend Kevin DeYoung, *What Does the Bible Really Teach about Homosexuality?* (Wheaton, IL: Crossway, 2015).

2. E.g., Denny Burk, "Suppressing the Truth in Unrighteousness: Matthew Vines Takes on the New Testament," in *God and the Gay Christian?: A Response to Matthew Vines*, ed. R. Albert Mohler Jr. (Louisville, KY: SBTS Press, 2014), 77–91; Denny Burk, *What Is the Meaning of Sex?* (Wheaton, IL: Crossway, 2013); Denny Burk, "Why Evangelicals Should Not Heed Brian McLaren: How the New Testament Requires Evangelicals to Render a Judgment on the Moral Status of Homosexuality," *Themelios* 35, no. 2 (2010): 212–26; Heath Lambert, "Is a 'Gay Christian' Consistent with the Gospel of Christ?," in Mohler, *God and the Gay Christian?*, 43–57.

3. One recent example of this is Kevin DeYoung's popular work *What Does the Bible Really Teach about Homosexuality?* (Wheaton, IL: Crossway, 2015).

4. Burk, *What Is the Meaning of Sex?*; Heath Lambert, *Finally Free: Fighting for Purity with the Power of Grace* (Grand Rapids: Zondervan, 2013).

5. This happened in the Supreme Court's long-awaited decision on gay marriage, *Obergefell v. Hodges*. Justices had two questions to

115

answer: (1) Does the Fourteenth Amendment require states to issue marriage licenses to two people of the same sex? (2) Does the Fourteenth Amendment require states to recognize same-sex marriages licensed in other states? A bare majority of justices answered yes to both questions. As a result, the Supreme Court requires all states to issue marriage licenses to gay couples. Gay marriage is now legal and *required* in all fifty states. Here's the actual language from the holding: "The Fourteenth Amendment requires a State to license a marriage between two people of the same sex and to recognize a marriage between two people of the same sex when their marriage was lawfully licensed and performed out-of-State."

Chapter One: What Is Same-Sex Attraction?

1. Herb Kutchins and Stuart Kirk, *Making Us Crazy: DSM: The Psychiatric Bible and the Creation of Mental Disorders* (New York: Free Press, 2003).

2. Rosaria Champagne Butterfield, *Openness Unhindered: Further Thoughts of an Unlikely Convert on Sexual Identity and Union with Christ* (Pittsburgh: Crown & Covenant, 2015), 96–97.

3. "Answers to Your Questions: For a Better Understanding of Sexual Orientation & Homosexuality," *American Psychological Association*, 2008, http://www.apa.org/topics/lgbt/orientation.pdf.

4. Indeed, there are many writers who reject the authority of Scripture (the "liberal" category below) who also adopt revisionist interpretations of Scripture (the "revisionist" category below).

5. Luke Timothy Johnson and Eve Tushnet, "Homosexuality and the Church: Two Views," *Commonweal*, June 15, 2007, 15. A recent popular example of this point of view is Brandon Ambrosino, "The Best Christian Argument for Marriage Equality Is That the Bible Got It Wrong," *Pacific Standard*, July 22, 2015, http://www.psmag.com/books-and-culture/jesus

-was-wrong-about-homosexuality. Ambrosino argues not only that the Bible is wrong but that Jesus himself was mistaken about homosexuality.

6. There are countless lines of argument in the literature offering revisionist interpretations. Those arguments have been ably refuted over the years (e.g., Robert A. J. Gagnon, *The Bible and Homosexual Practice: Texts and Hermeneutics* [Nashville, TN: Abingdon, 2001]). It is not our aim to engage that important polemical work in this book. We merely wish to note this common way of evading scriptural norms.

7. Matthew Vines, *God and the Gay Christian: The Biblical Case in Support of Same-Sex Relationships* (New York: Convergent, 2014), 130. In his book, Vines appears to be popularizing the work of James V. Brownson, *Bible, Gender, Sexuality: Reframing the Church's Debate on Same-Sex Relationships* (Grand Rapids: Eerdmans, 2013).

8. Denny Burk, "Suppressing the Truth in Unrighteousness: Matthew Vines Takes on the New Testament," in *God and the Gay Christian?: A Response to Matthew Vines*, ed. R. Albert Mohler Jr. (Louisville, KY: SBTS Press, 2014), 43–57; Heath Lambert, "Is a 'Gay Christian' Consistent with the Gospel of Christ?," in ibid., 77–91.

9. See http://spiritualfriendship.org/author/wahill/. The Spiritual Friendship site includes both Protestant and Roman Catholic writers. So the theological perspective there is certainly not monolithic. Even their views on this question are not monolithic. Nevertheless, there are many there who do not view same-sex attraction as necessarily sinful.

10. See Eve Tushnet, *Gay and Catholic: Accepting My Sexuality, Finding Community, Living My Faith* (Notre Dame, IN: Ave Maria, 2014).

11. Wesley Hill, "Is Being Gay Sanctifiable?," *Spiritual Friendship*, February 26, 2014, http://spiritualfriendship.org/2014/02/26/is-being-gay-sanctifiable/.

12. Wesley Hill, *Spiritual Friendship: Finding Love in the Church as a Celibate Gay Christian* (Grand Rapids: Brazos, 2015), 81.

13. We hope to demonstrate this in the next chapter.

14. It is sometimes claimed that sexual orientation is a modern concept that would have been completely foreign to the writers of Scripture. E.g., John Boswell, *Christianity, Social Tolerance, and Homosexuality: Gay People in Western Europe from the Beginning of the Christian Era to the Fourteenth Century* (Chicago: University of Chicago Press, 1980), 109, 117. Insofar as sexual orientation refers to a person's experience of sexual desire, this claim is certainly not true.

15. "Answers to Your Questions."

16. So DeYoung, *What Does the Bible Really Teach about Homosexuality?* (Wheaton, IL: Crossway, 2015), 147: "When people speak of 'orientation' or 'being gay,' they may be speaking of much more than sex. But we must also bear in mind that the world probably doesn't hear *less* than sex when we use these terms."

17. Simon LeVay, *Gay, Straight, and the Reason Why: The Science of Sexual Orientation* (New York: Oxford University Press, 2011), 1.

18. Edward Stein, *The Mismeasure of Desire: The Science, Theory, and Ethics of Sexual Orientation* (Oxford University Press, 1999), 40.

19. Mark A. Yarhouse and Erica S. N. Tan, *Sexuality and Sex Therapy: A Comprehensive Christian Appraisal* (Downers Grove, IL: InterVarsity, 2014), 296.

20. Sometimes we hear writers try to make a distinction between sexual "attraction" and sexual "desire." We do not find this to be a very compelling argument. The terms commonly appear as synonyms in the literature. That is clear from Yarhouse and Tan's definition of *orientation* quoted above. We could multiply other examples from the literature indicating that sexual "attraction" is used as a catch-all term for the erotic feelings that a person experiences for another person. For example, Hollinger

says that persons with homosexual orientation experience "ongoing affectional and sexual feelings toward persons of the same sex" (Dennis P. Hollinger, *The Meaning of Sex: Christian Ethics and the Moral Life* [Grand Rapids: Baker Academic, 2009], 172). Likewise, Grenz describes homosexual orientation as "the situation in which erotic feelings are nearly exclusively triggered by persons of one's own sex" (Stanley J. Grenz, *Sexual Ethics: An Evangelical Perspective* [Louisville, KY: Westminster John Knox, 1997], 225). See also Jenell Williams Paris's book in which three terms—*orientation*, *attraction*, and *desire*—are all used as virtual synonyms (Jenell Williams Paris, *The End of Sexual Identity: Why Sex Is Too Important to Define Who We Are* [Downers Grove, IL: InterVarsity, 2011], 99).

21. John S. Feinberg and Paul D. Feinberg, *Ethics for a Brave New World* (Wheaton, IL: Crossway, 1993), 385. So also James B. DeYoung, *Homosexuality: Contemporary Claims Examined in Light of the Bible and Other Ancient Literature and Law* (Grand Rapids: Kregel, 2000), 293–94: "Homosexual orientation was known in the generations in which Scripture was written. Paul gives no indication that it does not fall under the general condemnations of homosexuality in Romans 1, 1 Corinthians, and 1 Timothy."

22. Herman Bavinck, however, makes the case that the will is involved even in involuntary sins. His remarks to that end are profound, and we quote at length: "Though it is true that the voluntary element in this restricted sense is not always a constituent in the concept of sin, the sins of the human state and involuntary sins still do not totally occur apart from the will. There is not only an antecedent but also a concomitant, a consequent, and an approving will. Later, to a greater or lesser degree, the will approves of the sinfulness of our nature and takes delight in it. . . . It can be said that at the

most fundamental level all sin is voluntary. There is nobody or nothing that compels the sinner to serve sin. Sin is enthroned not outside the sinner but in the sinner and guides the sinner's thinking and desiring in its own direction. It is the sinner's sin insofar as the sinner has made it his or her own by means of his or her various faculties and powers" (Herman Bavinck, *Reformed Dogmatics*, ed. John Bolt, trans. John Vriend, vol. 3, *Sin and Salvation in Christ* [Grand Rapids: Baker, 2006], 144). Thanks to Tony Reinke for alerting us to this section in Bavinck's work.

23. As far as the science is concerned, it is not credible to be dogmatic as to what causes a particular sexual orientation. From a clinical perspective, the research simply does not allow one to land definitively on either nature or nurture. Mark Yarhouse and Erica Tan explain. "We do not know the causes of same-sex attractions or homosexual orientation (nor do we know the causes of attraction to the opposite-sex, as such). Most experts today seem to believe that sexual orientation is the result of many possible contributing factors, both from nature (broadly understood) and from nurture (also broadly under-stood). These factors are likely weighted differently for different people" (Yarhouse and Tan, *Sexuality and Sex Therapy*, 298–99).

See also "Answers to Your Questions": "There is no consensus among scientists about the exact reasons that an individual develops a heterosexual, bisexual, gay, or lesbian orientation. Although much research has examined the possible genetic, hormonal, developmental, social, and cultural influences on sexual orientation, no findings have emerged that permit scientists to conclude that sexual orientation is determined by any particular factor or factors. Many think that nature and nurture both play complex roles; most people experience little or no sense of choice about their sexual orientation."

So also, "Position Statement on Issues Related to Homosexuality," *American Psychiatric Association*, December 2013, http://
www.psychiatry.org/File%20Library/Learn/Archives
/Position-2013-Homosexuality.pdf: "The American Psychiatric Association believes that the causes of sexual orientation
(whether homosexual or heterosexual) are not known at this
time and likely are multifactorial including biological and
behavioral roots which may vary between different individuals
and may even vary over time."

24. Richard B. Hays, *The Moral Vision of the New Testament:
Community, Cross, New Creation, A Contemporary Introduction to
New Testament Ethics* (New York: HarperOne, 1996), 390. Hays
writes elsewhere, "Paul's condemnation of homosexual activity
does not rest upon an assumption that it is freely chosen;
indeed, it is precisely characteristic of Paul to regard 'sin' as a
condition of human existence, a condition which robs us of free
volition and drives us to disobedient actions which, though
involuntary, are nonetheless culpable. . . . The gulf is wide
between Paul's viewpoint and the modern habit of assigning
culpability only for actions assumed to be under free control of
the agent" (Richard B. Hays, "Relations Natural and Unnatural:
A Response to John Boswell's Exegesis of Romans 1," *Journal of
Religious Ethics* 14, no. 1 [Spring 1986]: 209).

25. Charles Hodge, *Systematic Theology* (New York: Charles
Scribner, 1872; repr., Peabody, MA: Hendrickson, 1999), 2:107.

26. Ibid., 110.

27. Ibid., 113.

28. Louis Berkhof explains, "Sin does not consist only in
overt acts, but also in sinful habits and in a sinful condition of the soul. . . . The sinful acts and dispositions of man
must be referred to and find their explanation in a corrupt
nature. . . . The state or condition of man is thoroughly

sinful. . . . In conclusion it may be said that sin may be defined
as *lack of conformity to the moral law of God, either in act,
disposition, or state*" (Louis Berkhof, *Systematic Theology*, new
combined ed. [Grand Rapids: Eerdmans, 1996], 233).

29. The doctrine of original sin in the Reformed tradition implies
a total depravity of human nature. This does not mean that any
particular sinner is as sinful as he could possibly be. It means
that every part of the sinner is polluted by sin and is therefore
inclined toward evil. John Calvin gives the classic formulation:
"Original sin, therefore, seems to be a hereditary depravity and
corruption of our nature, diffused into all parts of the soul,
which first makes us liable to God's wrath, then also brings
forth in us those works which Scripture calls 'works of the
flesh'. . . . We are so vitiated and perverted in every part of our
nature that by this great corruption we stand justly condemned
and convicted before God, to whom nothing is acceptable but
righteousness, innocence, and purity" (John Calvin, *Calvin:
Institutes of the Christian Religion*, ed. John T. McNeill, trans.
Ford Lewis Battles [Philadelphia: Westminster, 1960], 1:251).

30. John Owen's classic *The Nature and Power of Indwelling Sin* says
it this way: "I know no greater burden in the life of a believer
than these involuntary surprisals of soul; involuntary, I say, as
to the actual consent of the will, but not so in respect of that
corruption which is in the will, and is the principle of them. . . .
And this is the first thing in this lusting of the law of sin,—it
consists in its habitual propensity unto evil, manifesting itself
by the involuntary surprisals of the soul unto sin, and its read-
iness, without dispute or consideration, to join in all temptations whatever" (John Owen, "The Nature, Power, Deceit, and
Prevalency of the Remainders of Indwelling Sin in Believers," in
The Works of John Owen, vol. 6, *Temptation and Sin* [repr., Edinburgh: Banner of Truth, 1967], 153–322).

31. Hill, *Spiritual Friendship*, 80.

32. Wesley Hill, "Is Being Gay Sanctifiable?"

33. This is the question that Wesley Hill asks in his aforementioned essay. See Hill, "Is Being Gay Sanctifiable?"

34. Anthony Esolen argues that the loss of a stigma on homosexual relationships has had a deleterious effect on male friendships. It places all male friendships in a frame of sexual possibility that didn't exist in previous generations. He writes, "The stigma against sodomy cleared away ample space for an emotionally powerful friendship that did not involve sexual intercourse, exactly as the stigma against incest allows for the physical and emotional freedom of a family" (Anthony Esolen, *Defending Marriage: Twelve Arguments for Sanity* [Charlotte, NC: Saint Benedict, 2014], 66).

35. Hanne Blank, *Straight: The Surprisingly Short History of Heterosexuality* (Boston: Beacon, 2012), 4.

36. Jonathan Katz argues that heterosexual orientation is a social construction of late modernity. See Jonathan Ned Katz, *The Invention of Heterosexuality* (Chicago: University of Chicago Press, 1995), 18.

37. Michael W. Hannon, "Against Heterosexuality," *First Things*, March 2014, 28.

38. Ibid.

39. Ibid., 33.

40. Sam Allberry, *Is God Anti-Gay? And Other Questions about Homosexuality, the Bible and Same-Sex Attraction* (Purcellville, VA: The Good Book Company, 2013), 8–9, 30.

41. Mark Yarhouse argues that gay identity is a self-understanding that is defined by one's sexual attractions. Moreover, gay identity involves *assent* to those attractions and to the behaviors that stem from those attractions. He writes, "With the swinging of the pendulum toward identity comes the conclusion that

all things homosexual are good and all things heterosexual are questionable" (Mark A. Yarhouse, *Homosexuality and the Christian: A Guide for Parents, Pastors, and Friends* [Minneapolis, MN: Bethany House, 2010], 46). See also 44–50.

42. Butterfield, *Openness Unhindered*, 106.

Chapter Two: Is Same-Sex Attraction Sinful?

1. A version of this essay appears in Denny Burk, "Is Homosexual Orientation Sinful?," *The Journal of the Evangelical Theological Society* 58, no. 1 (March 2015): 95–115.

2. See "Desire Strongly" in Johannes P. Louw and Eugene A. Nida, eds., *Greek-English Lexicon of the New Testament Based on Semantic Domains* (New York: United Bible Societies, 1988), 1:290–92.

3. Augustine's thought on the nature of indwelling sin appears to have changed over time, and this change was due in large part to a shift in his interpretation of Romans 7. See Eugene TeSelle, "Exploring the Inner Conflict: Augustine's Sermons on Romans 7 and 8," in *Augustine: Biblical Exegete*, ed. Frederick Van Fleteren and Joseph C. Schnaubelt, Collectanea Augustiniana (New York: Peter Lang, 2001), 313.

Christopher Bounds describes the change this way: "In 395 Augustine acknowledges that a Christian still experiences the lusts of the flesh, but does not sin. At this point in his theology, he defines sin as the consent of the will to obey, or to act according to sinful desire. Simply having sinful desire is not personal sin. . . . However, by the opening decades of the fifth century, Augustine's hamartiology expands. He begins to see sinful desire itself as personal sin and in need of the absolution brought about through the Lord's Prayer. . . . While he only sees it as venial sin and not mortal, it is still sin that a Christian must bear until the resurrection of the body. Augustine comes to see sinful desire as sin because it falls short of the perfect love of God and neighbor, which is the ultimate end of the law" (Christopher T. Bounds, "Augustine's Interpretation of Romans 7:14–25, His *Ordo Salutis* and His Consistent Belief in a Christian's Victory over Sin," *The Asbury Journal* 64, no. 2 [2009]: 24).

4. In sermon 155, Augustine explains "why concupiscence is called sin" ["Concupiscentia cur vocetur peccatum"]. He writes, "In concluding like that, the apostle showed why he said what he had said above: *Now it is no longer I that perform it, but the sin that lives in me* (Rom. 7:20); it was because he wasn't performing it by consenting with the mind, but by lusting with the flesh. He gives the name of sin, you see, to that from which all sins spring, namely to the lust [concupiscence] of the flesh" (Saint Augustine, "Sermon 155: On the Words of the Apostle, Romans 8:1–11: There Is Therefore No Condemnation Now for Those Who Are in Christ Jesus, Etc. Against the Pelagians, Preached in the Basilica of the Holy Scillitan Martyrs," in *Sermons*, trans. Edmund Hill, vol. 5, *148–183* [New Rochelle, NY: New City Press, 1992], 84).

5. Saint Augustine, "Sermon 151: On the Words of the Apostle, Romans 7:15–25: For It Is Not the Good I Want to That I Do, but the Evil I Do Not Want To, That Is What I Do, Etc.," in Hill, *Sermons*, 42.

6. Augustin, "On Marriage and Concupiscence," in *St. Augustin: Anti-Pelagian Writings*, ed. Philip Schaff, Nicene and Post-Nicene Fathers of the Christian Church 5 (Peabody, MA: Hendrickson, 2004), 274. In sections 1.1, 8.7, and 9.8 of the same work, Augustine repeatedly refers to the "evil of concupiscence."

7. The *Catechism of the Catholic Church* (section 2515) is clear on this point: "Etymologically, 'concupiscence' can refer to any intense form of human desire. Christian theology has given it a particular meaning: the movement of the sensitive appetite

contrary to the operation of the human reason. The apostle St. Paul identifies it with the rebellion of the 'flesh' against the 'spirit.' Concupiscence stems from the disobedience of the first sin. It unsettles man's moral faculties and, without being in itself an offense, inclines man to commit sins" (Catholic Church, *Catechism of the Catholic Church: Revised in Accordance With the Official Latin Text Promulgated by Pope John Paul II*, 2nd ed. [Washington, D.C.: Libreria Editrice Vaticana, 2000], 602).

Lisa Cahill argues that the Roman Catholic tradition on sexual desire developed more in line with Aquinas than with Augustine. See Lisa Sowle Cahill, "Using Augustine in Contemporary Sexual Ethics: A Response to Gilbert Meilaender," *Journal of Religious Ethics* 29, no. 1 (Spring 2001): 27.

8. Catholic Church, *Catechism of the Catholic Church* (sections 2357 and 2358), 566.

9. Bavinck's discussion of the variant trajectories of Roman Catholicism and the Reformed tradition on this point is extremely helpful. See Herman Bavinck, *Reformed Dogmatics*, ed. John Bolt, trans. John Vriend, vol. 3, *Sin and Salvation in Christ* (Grand Rapids: Baker, 2006), 142–44.

10. John Calvin, *The Institutes of the Christian Religion*, trans. Henry Beveridge, vol. 1 (Grand Rapids: Eerdmans, 1957), 517. See also the Battles translation of the *Institutes* at 2.1.8 on concupiscence: "Those who have said that original sin is 'concupiscence' have used an appropriate word, if only it be added—something that most will by no means concede—that whatever is in man, from the understanding to the will, from the soul even to the flesh, has been defiled and crammed with this concupiscence. Or, to put it more briefly, the whole man is of himself nothing but concupiscence" (John Calvin, *Calvin: Institutes of the Christian Religion*, ed. John T. McNeill, trans. Ford Lewis Battles [Philadelphia: Westminster, 1960], 252). See also *Institutes* 2.7.5.

Gregg Allison writes, "These versions of evangelical theology dissent from this [Roman Catholic] position, insisting that fallen human nature, which produces the tendency to sin (concupiscence), is an aspect of original sin and thus incurs the wrath of God" (Gregg R. Allison, *Roman Catholic Theology & Practice: An Evangelical Assessment* [Wheaton, IL: Crossway, 2014], 130). See also Barbara Pitkin, "Nothing But Concupiscence: Calvin's Understanding of Sin and the Via Augustini," *Calvin Theological Journal* 34, no. 2 (November 1999): 358.

11. Sin is defined not as *intentional* transgression of God's law but as *any* transgression of God's law. That is why the law of Moses requires sacrifices even for sins committed unintentionally (Lev. 4:1–5:13). Falling short of God's righteous standard is sinful whether we realize it or not. Note question 14 of the Westminster Shorter Catechism: "Q: What is sin? A: Sin is any want of conformity unto, or transgression of, the law of God."

12. R. T. France's translation is very specific on this point: "Every man who looks at someone else's wife and wants to have sex with her has already committed adultery with her in his heart" (R. T. France, *The Gospel of Matthew*, The New International Commentary on the New Testament [Grand Rapids: Eerdmans, 2007], 192).

13. By this, we mean Matthew's account of Jesus' words. Matthew's account is in Greek, but it is widely agreed that Jesus actually spoke Aramaic. Nevertheless, Matthew's account establishes intertextual connections with the Greek version of the Ten Commandments. I believe that Matthew faithfully represents Jesus' intention in making these connections.

14. The *Greek-English Lexicon* (hereafter referred to as BDAG) confirms that the preponderance of this term's use in the New Testament means simply "desire," not "lust." See Walter Bauer, *A Greek-English Lexicon of the New Testament and Other Early*

Christian Literature, rev. and ed. Frederick William Danker, 3rd ed. (Chicago: University of Chicago Press, 2000), s.v. "ἐπιθυμέω" 1: "to have a strong desire to do or secure someth., *desire, long for.*"

15. The intensity of desire is not an irrelevant moral consideration. An overly intense desire for a good object may indicate the presence of idolatry in the heart. Having said that, the intensity of desire is not the first moral consideration in Jesus' words in Matthew 5:27–28. A low-level desire for an evil object is always an evil desire. The intensity of the desire—no matter how slight—does not change that fundamental moral precept. In Matthew 5:27–28, Jesus is not excusing low-level sexual desire for another man's wife. In keeping with the Tenth Command-ment, he is prohibiting *any* sexual desire for another man's wife. In this case, the object of the desire is the defining moral concern, not the intensity of the desire.

16. BDAG's discussion of ἐπιθυμία is based entirely upon the object of desire. If the object of desire is neutral or positive, then ἐπιθυμία is translated as "desire, longing, craving" (e.g., Mark 4:19; Luke 22:15; Phil. 1:23; 1 Thess. 2:17; Rev. 18:14). If the object of desire is negative/sinful, then ἐπιθυμία is to be translated as "craving, lust" (e.g., Rom. 7:7; Col. 3:5; James 1:14; 2 Pet. 1:4). See also DeYoung, *What Does the Bible Really Teach about Homosexuality?* (Wheaton, IL: Crossway, 2015), 145: "Desires are deemed good or bad not just by their intensity or sense of proportion, but based on their object."

17. The NET Bible's note on this text indicates that the same dynamic is in play for the underlying Hebrew term for "desire": "The verb חָמַד (*khamad*) focuses not on an external act but on an internal mental activity behind the act, the motivation for it. The word can be used in a very good sense (Ps 19:10; 68:16), but it has a bad connotation in contexts where the object desired is off limits. This command is aimed at curtailing the greedy desire for something belonging to a neighbor, a desire that leads

to the taking of it or the attempt to take it. It was used in the
story of the Garden of Eden for the tree that was desired" (note
on Exodus 20:17 in *The NET Bible*).

18. So also Craig S. Keener, *The Gospel of Matthew: A Socio-Rhetorical
Commentary* (Grand Rapids: Eerdmans, 2009), 189: "By saying
'adultery' Jesus technically addresses only lust for married
women . . . but this is an example that should provoke its hearers
to consider related moral issues. Thus, for example, it rules out
'fornication of the heart' as well; Israelite law treated premarital
sex in part as an offense against one's future spouse and one's
partner's future spouse (Deut. 22:13–21)."

19. Denny Burk, *What Is the Meaning of Sex?* (Wheaton, IL:
Crossway, 2013), 43–59. See also Burk's discussion of teleology
and the purposes of sex on pp. 31–40.

20. See BDAG, s.v. "πειράζω," 2.b.

21. E.g., Peter T. O'Brien, *The Letter to the Hebrews*, Pillar New
Testament Commentary (Grand Rapids: Eerdmans, 2010),
183. See also Paul Ellingworth, *The Epistle to the Hebrews*, New
International Greek Testament Commentary (Grand Rapids:
Eerdmans, 1993), 268–69: "This verse recalls 2:18, the only other
place in which Hebrews uses πειράζω of Christ, and there
πειρασθείς is related to his suffering (πέπονθεν), and by impli-
cation to his death. The same connection recurs in 5:7, though
without the use of πειράζω, so an implicit allusion to the final
test of the cross is possible, as perhaps in 12:4 (cf. 12:2)."

22. Greek: καθ᾽ ὁμοιότητα.

23. As quoted in O'Brien, *The Letter to the Hebrews*, 184.

24. Louis Berkhof defines Christ's impeccability: "This means not
merely that Christ could avoid sinning (*potuit non peccare*), and
did actually avoid it, but also that it was impossible for Him to
sin (*non potuit peccare*) because of the essential bond between
the human and the divine natures. . . . While Christ was made to

be sin judicially, yet ethically He was free from both hereditary depravity and actual sin" (Louis Berkhof, *Systematic Theology*, new combined ed. [Grand Rapids: Eerdmans, 1996], 318).

So also Wayne Grudem, *Systematic Theology: An Introduction to Biblical Doctrine* (Grand Rapids: Zondervan, 1994), 539: "If we are asking if it was *actually* possible for Jesus to have sinned, it seems that we must conclude that it was not possible. The union of his human and divine natures in one person prevented it."

25. Augustin, "A Treatise on Nature and Grace," in *St. Augustin: Anti-Pelagian Writings*, 115–51.

26. Leon Morris, *The Lord From Heaven: A Study of the New Testament Teaching on the Deity and Humanity of Jesus* (Grand Rapids: Eerdmans, 1958), 51–52, quoted in Millard J. Erickson, *Christian Theology*, 2nd ed. (Grand Rapids: Baker, 1998), 737.

27. It is not sinful to be hungry or to eat bread. The temptation had to do with procuring the bread on Satan's terms rather than on God's. So John Calvin, *Commentary on a Harmony of the Evangelists, Matthew, Mark and Luke, vol. 1*, trans. William Pringle, Calvin's Commentaries (repr., Grand Rapids: Baker, 1999), 213–14.

28. Douglas J. Moo, *The Letter of James*, Pillar New Testament Commentary (Grand Rapids: Eerdmans, 2000), 74.

29. John Owen, "The Nature, Power, Deceit, and Prevalency of the Remainders of Indwelling Sin in Believers," in *The Works of John Owen*, vol. 6, *Temptation and Sin* (repr., Edinburgh: Banner of Truth, 1967), 194. In that same passage, Owen defines what temptation is *vis a vis* desire: "Now, what is it to be tempted? It is to have that proposed to a man's consideration which, if he close withal, it is evil, it is sin unto him. This is sin's trade: Ἐπιθυμεῖ—'It lusteth.' It is raising up in the heart, and proposing unto the mind and affections, that which is evil; trying, as it were, whether the soul will close with its

suggestions, or how far it will carry them on, though it do not wholly prevail" (ibid.).

30. Special thanks to our colleague Rob Plummer who read an early draft of this chapter and who raised this thoughtful objection with us in a private email.

31. BDAG confirms this range of meaning for the term. Meaning 1 in BDAG focuses on sinful deeds. Meanings 2 and 3 focus on sin as "a state of being sinful" and "a destructive evil power" within the sinner. See BDAG, s.v. "ἁμαρτία."

32. Sam Allberry, *James For You* (Purcellville, VA: The Good Book Company, 2015), 34–35.

33. E.g., *The New Hampshire Baptist Confession*, section 3: "All mankind are now sinners, not by constraint, but choice; being by nature utterly void of that holiness required by the law of God, positively inclined to evil" (John Newton Brown, "The New Hampshire Baptist Confession," 1833, available online at http://www.spurgeon.org/~phil/creeds/nh_conf.htm). The authors of this book are Southern Baptist, and our own denomination's faith statement says it this way: "Through the temptation of Satan man transgressed the command of God, and fell from his original innocence whereby his posterity inherit a nature and an environment inclined toward sin" (Southern Baptist Convention, "The 2000 Baptist Faith & Message," section 3, available online at http://www.sbc.net/bfm2000 /bfm2000.asp).

34. As John Owen has famously said, "Be killing sin or it will be killing you" (John Owen, "Of the Mortification of Sin in Believers," in *Temptation and Sin*, The Works of John Owen 6 [Edinburgh: Banner of Truth, 1967], 9).

35. Mark A. Yarhouse, *Homosexuality and the Christian: A Guide for Parents, Pastors, and Friends* (Minneapolis, MN: Bethany House, 2010), 93–95.

Chapter Three: Myths about Change

1. One example of this is from the ministry of W. A. Criswell, a preacher of massive influence in the last century. In one sermon, "Why God Abhors the Homosexual," preached in May of 1986, Criswell expounded several Scriptures that clearly condemn homosexuality. He spent a good bit of his sermon expressing shock and amazement at the cultural trend to embrace homosexuality. He concluded his sermon with an appeal to embrace a biblical sexuality by falling in love with someone of the opposite sex and developing a good, Christian home. We are thankful for Criswell's exemplary ministry, and we share his position on the sinfulness of homosexuality. This is a common example, however, of the unfortunate absence of any teaching concerning how to change. See W. A. Criswell, "Why God Abhors the Homosexual" (sermon, May 28, 1986), available online at http://www.wacriswell.com/transcript /?thisid=F192DD3C-6FF4-4A8D-B9CF6B0A08E15537.

2. Matthew Vines, *God and the Gay Christian: The Biblical Case in Support of Same-Sex Relationships* (New York: Convergent, 2014), 2.

3. Heath Lambert, "Is a 'Gay Christian' Consistent with the Gospel of Christ?," in *God and the Gay Christian?: A Response to Matthew Vines*, ed. R. Albert Mohler Jr. (Louisville, KY: SBTS Press, 2014), 88–89; Denny Burk, *What Is the Meaning of Sex?* (Wheaton, IL: Crossway, 2013), 198–200.

4. *Sing Over Me*, directed by Jacob Kindberg (Worcester, PA: Vision Video, 2014), DVD.

5. There have been several studies over the years attempting to document whether sexual orientation can change. See summary in Mark A. Yarhouse, *Homosexuality and the Christian: A Guide for Parents, Pastors, and Friends* (Minneapolis, MN: Bethany House, 2010), 83–90. In 2007, Mark Yarhouse and Stanton Jones completed a study of 98 persons attempting to change their

sexual orientation. Here's how Yarhouse summarizes their findings: "Participants were categorized on the information they shared about their change efforts. Fifteen percent fell into the category of *Success: Conversion* (to heterosexuality); 23 percent landed in the category of *Success: Chastity* (or the 'freedom to live chaste,' which was helped by a reduction in same-sex attraction); and 2 percent of the participants were categorized as *Continuing change effort*, which meant there was some reduction in attraction but not enough to describe themselves as having experienced success. In addition, 15 percent of the participants were designated as having *No Response* to change effort; 4 percent as *Failure: Confused*; and 8 percent as *Failure: Gay Identity*. The designations of 'failure' were only with reference to the goals of the participants themselves, in terms of being a part of Exodus to experience a change in attractions or orientation" (ibid., 88).

6. "California Becomes First State in Nation to Ban 'Gay Cure' Therapy for Children," *NBC News*, September 30, 2012, http://usnews.nbcnews.com/_news/2012/09/30/14159337-california-becomes-first-state-in-nation-to-ban-gay-cure-therapy-for-children.

7. Valerie Jarrett, "Response to Your Petition on Conversion Therapy," *The White House President Barack Obama*, April 8, 2015, https://petitions.whitehouse.gov/response/response-your-petition-conversion-therapy.

8. For more information on the problems of reparative therapy, see Heath Lambert, "What's Wrong with Reparative Therapy," *Association of Certified Biblical Counselors*, November 17, 2014, http://www.biblicalcounseling.com/blog/what-wrong-with-reparative-therapy.

9. J. R. Daling et al., "Correlates of Homosexual Behavior and Increased Anal Cancer," *The Journal of the American Medical Association* 247, no. 14 (April 1982): 1988–90.

10. Jeffrey Satinover, *Homosexuality and the Politics of Truth* (Grand Rapids: Baker, 1996), 69.

11. J. M. Bailey, "Homosexuality and Mental Illness," *Archives of General Psychiatry* 56, no. 10 (October 1999): 883–84.

12. Justin Lee, *Torn: Rescuing the Gospel from the Gays-Vs.-Christians Debate* (New York: Jericho, 2012), 38–39.

13. Joseph J. Nicolosi, *Shame and Attachment Loss: The Practical Work of Reparative Therapy* (Downers Grove, IL: InterVarsity, 2009), 324.

14. Ibid., 69.

15. Ibid., 150.

Chapter Four: A Biblical Path to Change

1. Julie Roys, "Wheaton's 'gay celibate Christian,'" *WORLD*, December 11, 2014, http://www.worldmag.com/2014/12/wheaton_s_gay_celibate_christian.

2. Julie Rodgers, "An Update on the Gay Debate: Evolving Ideas, Untidy Stories, and Hopes for the Church," *Julie Rodgers* (blog), July 15, 2015, https://julierodgers.wordpress.com/2015/07/13/an-update-on-the-gay-debate-evolving-ideas-untidy-stories-and-hopes-for-the-church/.

3. Walter Bauer, *A Greek-English Lexicon of the New Testament and Other Early Christian Literature*, rev. and ed. Frederick William Danker, 3rd ed. (Chicago: University of Chicago Press, 2000), s.v. "πλεονεξία": "the state of desiring to have more than one's due, *greediness, insatiableness, avarice, covetousness.*"

4. For more on taking radical steps to uproot your sin see Heath Lambert, *Finally Free: Fighting for Purity with the Power of Grace* (Grand Rapids: Zondervan, 2013), 59–74.

5. For further explanation on Bible reading and prayer as the means of abiding, see Robert Cheong and Heath Lambert, "The Goal and Focus of Spiritual Formation," in *Christ-Centered Biblical Counseling: Changing Lives with God's Changeless Truth,*

ed. James MacDonald, Bob Kellemen, and Steve Viars (Eugene, OR: Harvest House, 2013), 285–96.

6. Rosaria Champagne Butterfield, *The Secret Thoughts of an Unlikely Convert: An English Professor's Journey into Christian Faith* (Pittsburgh, PA: Crown & Covenant, 2012), 86–87. Though many readers certainly disagree with her denomination's focus on Psalms-only worship, Butterfield has rightly grasped the power for change that happens when one regularly sings the truths of Scripture.

Chapter Five: How Evangelicals Can Change

1. Much of what follows is a substantial revision of Denny Burk, "How Do We Speak about Homosexuality?," *The Journal for Biblical Manhood & Womanhood* 17, no. 1 (Spring 2012): 31–37. Used by permission.

2. Wesley Hill, *Washed and Waiting: Reflections on Christian Faithfulness and Homosexuality* (Grand Rapids: Zondervan, 2010), 61.

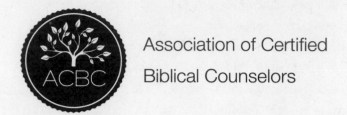

Association of Certified
Biblical Counselors

Since 1976, the Association of Certified Biblical Counselors (ACBC) has been certifying biblical counselors to ensure doctrinal integrity and to promote excellence in biblical counseling. We offer a comprehensive biblical counseling certification program that is rigorous, but attainable by even the busiest pastor or church member. Our certification process is made up of three phases: learning, exams and application, and supervision.

The association has grown from a handful of certified counselors to obtaining a membership in the thousands. Now in our fourth decade of pursuing excellence in biblical counseling, we have had five executive directors: Dr. Bob Smith, Dr. Howard Eyrich, Rev. Bill Goode, and Rev. Randy Patten. Dr. Heath Lambert became the fifth executive director in 2013.

Every Christian is called to speak the truth in love to one another. ACBC trains Christians in their gospel responsibility to be disciple-makers and to build up the body of Christ. This training is accomplished through conferences and events throughout the world. ACBC has members in every state in America and counselors in sixteen different countries.

For more information about ACBC and biblical counseling resources, visit www.biblicalcounseling.com.